STRESS
FREE
KIDS®

STRESS FREE KIDS®

A Parent's Guide to Helping Build Self-Esteem, Manage Stress, and Reduce Anxiety in Children

LORI LITE, founder of Stress Free Kids®

Published by
Adams Media, a division of F+W Media, Inc.
57 Littlefield Street, Avon, MA 02322. U.S.A.
www.adamsmedia.com

ISBN 10: 1-4405-6751-4
ISBN 13: 978-1-4405-6751-3
eISBN 10: 1-4405-6752-2
eISBN 13: 978-1-4405-6752-0

Printed in the United States of America.

10   9   8   7   6   5   4   3   2   1

Library of Congress Cataloging-in-Publication Data

Lite, Lori.
  Stress free kids® / Lori Lite.
     pages cm
  Includes index.
  ISBN-13: 978-1-4405-6751-3 (pb)
  ISBN-10: 1-4405-6751-4 (pb)
  ISBN-13: 978-1-4405-6752-0 (ebk)
  ISBN-10: 1-4405-6752-2 (ebk)
  1. Stress in children. 2. Parenting. 3. Stress management for children. I. Title.
  BF723.S75L58 2014
  155.4'189042--dc23
                              2013034698

Stress Free Kids® is a registered trademark of Lori Lite.

This book is available at quantity discounts for bulk purchases.
For information, please call 1-800-289-0963.

ACKNOWLEDGMENTS

I am grateful to my children and husband for joining me on my parenting and writing journey. Their willingness to share intimate details of our stress recovery with others is an act of love that I am privileged to share in this book.

CONTENTS

PART III: STRESSFUL SITUATIONS, SOLVED ... 119

INTRODUCTION

Peaceful Parenting

"Smile, breathe, and go slowly."

—THICH NHAT HANH

You all know that's easier said than done, but you've come to this book because you're ready to make a change. You want a better, more relaxed life for your family—especially your kids.

This book's mission is to give you the tools that you need to help your children self-soothe, help your children manage the stress and anxiety that comes along with twenty-first-century life, help your children sleep more peacefully—and most important, help your children believe in themselves.

The aim of this book is to offer you parenting solutions to everyday stressors. These solutions will empower you and your children to actively participate in creating your own stress-free moments; think of them as a collection of moments that result in the freedom to live more peacefully. It's possible, and it only requires awareness and the willingness to integrate some simple relaxation techniques into your daily routine.

Your Go-To Tools: Breathing and Positive Statements

You were born breathing so it is already available to you—it's effortless and involuntary. If you watch a relaxed baby breathe, their little bellies rise up and down with each inhalation and exhalation. This is how you are designed to breathe and it's also how you naturally took in air—that is, before you began to experience stress.

Diaphragmatic—or belly—breathing is an easy, effective tool to teach your children. In fact, little ones embrace this method of breathing with less effort than adults. It's probably because children still remember their baby-breathing days. In this book, you'll discover how to pass on this valuable stress-reduction technique to your children.

Like belly breathing, positive statements can dramatically minimize the negative effects of stress. Consider this: Self-talk can reduce anxiety *or increase it* in mere seconds. The talking committee in your head can beat you down with criticism or lift you up with praise. Children, tweens, teens, and adults are all experts at self-criticism.

Ask anyone to make a list of their shortcomings versus their assets and you will get a much longer list of self-criticisms. We are so hard on ourselves. This causes stress and undermines our self-value.

However, children are less embarrassed than adults to show themselves love through positive statements. You can likely close your eyes and hear an entire classroom of children shouting, "I LOVE myself!" But it's much harder to picture a roomful of adults enthusiastically proclaiming the same thing. You may *try* to adopt a positive point of view, but a negative tone unconsciously tinges your affirmations. For example, instead of saying, "I will NOT yell today," you can bump up the positivity factor by saying, "Today, I will respond with a calm voice." Even reading those two statements should feel different to you. Try saying them quietly to yourself and out loud. Notice which way affects you at the deepest level. How enlightening it is to know which way works for you. It's truly that easy.

Both of these techniques help you to feel good and reduce stress on the spot. Immediate gratification. Children feel the effect right away; they recognize it feels good and want to do it again. *Voilà!* Stress-free moments created.

It is never too soon for a child to reap the benefits of relaxation and stress management. There are reports that state that stress levels during pregnancy can affect an unborn child. I used deep breathing throughout my last pregnancy and I believe that my newborn was easier to soothe because of this. In general, age 4 is when a child can start to participate in relaxation exercises, but I have seen children as young as 18 months copy breathing and positive statements. Little exposures and creating a familiarity around relaxation can begin at any age.

Imagine . . .

. . . children counteracting the stress and trauma of today's world.

Today's children are exposed to unprecedented types of stress. Children are aware of events like terrorism, kidnappings, natural disasters, and many have family members or a parent deployed. Stress-related conditions are considered to be a national epidemic and bullying tactics have reached new heights. Incidents of child and teen suicide have seen record numbers.

Achievement-oriented parenting has placed extra demands on our children. Today's children are running a stressful race that never ends. Pressure to excel at home, school, sports, and extracurricular activities creates a constant high-stress environment with no downtime. We think the child that manages the most activities while completing homework and maintaining high grades wins. But what do our children win at the end of the race?

Stress has been attributed to health issues ranging from high blood pressure to depression. The range of stress children experience can be as simple as arriving at school to find a substitute teacher for the day or as complex as being exposed to a violent image or experience. Stress-related symptoms in children can include—but are not limited to—unusual clingy behavior, sleep disturbances, physical complaints of headaches and stomachaches, and of course, rapid, shallow breathing. All of the resources and solutions have been focused on adults, but what about the children? There are scores of books designed to help adults manage their stress through relaxation and meditation. For the first time, we as a society are acknowledging that children are vulnerable to stress. The same techniques that have helped adults are now available to help children unwind, de-stress, and sleep peacefully. How different could your child's life be if he was aware of the power of breathing and knew how to turn negative thoughts into positive ones?

Imagine . . .

. . . reading a book to your child that shows him how to manage his range of emotions and grow his self-esteem.

Visualize the wave of tranquility that spreads through your family. Envision your feeling of satisfaction as you watch your child's self-esteem grow as he practices his affirmations. You will be inspired to see how easy it is for your child to apply breathing, visualizations, affirmations, and muscle relaxation to his life. Children have the ability to be active participants in creating their own healthy, peaceful lives. Children want to feel calm and in control of their minds and bodies. Children want to feel good!

Imagine . . .

. . . weaving a web of mindful moments that encourage your children to counteract stress, anxiety, and anger.

Today's children are overstimulated by technology, media, and even noise. Our children are making their way in a world that has dramatically changed. More than kids of days past, today's children are spending more time in school, in front of screens, and in structured settings such as daycare. Their fast-processing, multidimensional minds and bodies are expected to sit still and be excited by methods of teaching that need updating. The media bombards them with complicated, and potentially traumatizing images. Without complete vigilance to a media blackout, children soak in these messages. It has become necessary to counteract this by teaching our children stress- and anxiety-management techniques.

Imagine . . .

. . . a generation of children living longer, healthier, calmer lives than us, their parents.

My own stressful life journey sent me in search of ways to first help myself, and then my children. I learned that by simply adding deep belly breathing, affirmations, progressive muscle relaxation, and visualizations to my life, I could counteract the harmful effects stress was having on my body and mind. These techniques worked so well for me I wondered how my children would respond. I began to develop stories designed to entertain my children while at the same time introduce them to lifelong stress-management skills. I watched my young son follow along with *A Boy and a Bear* (*Indigo Dreams* CD) as he put his hands on his belly and learned diaphragmatic breathing. My daughter's night terrors disappeared as she repeated positive statements with the animals of the forest in *The Affirmation Web* (*Indigo Dreams* CD). The myriad benefits my family experienced by integrating stress-management techniques into our lives inspired me to continue creating stories to assist other parents looking for a way to help their children. How different could your child's life be if he knew how to slow down, relax, and see things more clearly?

That's exactly what you'll discover in the pages of this book.

PART I

THE STRESS CONNECTION

"For fast-acting relief, try slowing down."
—LILY TOMLIN

CHAPTER 1

Relaxed Parents

=

Relaxed Kids

*"In the happiest of our childhood memories,
our parents were happy, too."*

—ROBERT BRAULT

ᏣᏗ LORI'S LESSON ᏣᏗ

I became very sick from stress while I was raising my young children. My son was hyperactive and it took me two hours every single night to get him to fall sleep. At the same time my daughter developed stress-related night terrors. This created a tremendous amount of stress for my entire family. My husband and I were fighting about who was going to put our son to bed, and nobody was getting any sleep. Fortunately, this experience was the catalyst for me to find solutions for my own stress and inspired me to write stress-management stories to help my own children.

Helping your kids reduce stress in their lives begins with a stress-free you. Parents who practice stress-management techniques send a positive, calming ripple effect throughout the family. The first step entails looking at your stress levels and working to minimize them.

> *Imagine . . .*
> Close your eyes, take a deep breath, and imagine what it would feel like to be a peaceful parent.

Secure Your Own Serenity First

Parenting is one of the hardest roles to play. When coupled with jobs, household responsibilities, and the pressure to "keep up" or "keep it together," it's no wonder you feel like you're carrying a mountain of stress along with you as you move through your days! These stressors take a toll even on the best of parents, in fact, just trying to be a "perfect" parent can leave you feeling wound tight and short on patience—as opposed to open and relaxed—which can lead to knee-jerk reactivity or saying things in the home that don't contribute to creating the loving, carefree environment you desire. Unfortunately, your children absorb your stress; they are affected by how you respond when you're in a constrictive state. They learn how to respond to life by modeling how you respond. When you learn how to implement a pause, you start to shift from reacting to responding.

—— Relax FAQ ——

Q: Will my own stress affect my kids? How can I handle that?

A: Stress is contagious. If one person in the house is stressed-out it will affect everybody. The good news is relaxation and calm are also contagious. If you are stressed-out and you are seeing that it's affecting your children, the best thing you can do is acknowledge that you are stressed-out—be a good example! Tell your children, "I am feeling too stressed right now. I am just going to take a minute for myself to sit down and do my breathing." Your child can sit next to you and do some deep breathing with you. It is such a gift to be able to identify your stress, acknowledge it, and then share with your children that you can manage it, you can take it down a notch, you can make yourself feel good again, you can control yourself . . . Breathe in, 2, 3, 4, and out, 2, 3, 4. Children see you changing your energy and they want to experience it along with you.

In order to help your child enjoy the benefits of a relaxed life, you first have to find ways to cope with your own stress levels and minimize your reaction to them. And here's the good news: It's NEVER too late to make a positive change. You can't change the past, so it's no use expending energy on worry or regret. And the future has not yet arrived, so planning how you'll act differently does nothing to impact your life at this moment. Now—this present moment—is the only thing that matters! Now is the time you can make life dramatically better for yourself and your kids. All of your power is now. Not yesterday, not tomorrow, only now.

Are you ready to take a look at your stress? Take this quick quiz:

- Are you cramming more activities than you are comfortable with into a day?
- Are you saying "yes" to requests you wish you hadn't?
- Are you sleeping less?

- Do you find yourself yelling at your kids more?
- Are you forgetting things and misplacing your keys?
- Are you spending more money that you want to?
- Is there a change in your routine?
- Do you feel like you are living mostly out of your car?
- Are fast food restaurants your primary source of meals?
- Are you getting sick more often?

A "yes" answer to any of the above questions indicates an increase in stress. If you are experiencing an increase in stress then so are your children. An article published by the American Academy of Pediatrics points out that "many parents believe that their school-age children are unaware of the stresses around them and are somehow immune to them."

Parent's POV
On Raising Happy, Stress-Free Kids
"I hear you basically saying that in order for our kids to be stress-free, parents have to be stress free first. When I stress, it stresses my kids, even at 8, 11, and 14. The only difference when they are older is that they tell you that you are stressing them! Breathe deep. Relax. Enjoy. Pray. When I can step out of the stress, my kids step out of it too." —Janis

The Effects of Stress

Stress has reached epidemic levels. Unchecked, it manifests as "disease" or imbalance, with detrimental effects on your mind, body, and spirit. Some less noticeable symptoms might be:

- Mood swings
- Inability to sleep

- Feelings of depression and powerlessness
- Inability to concentrate
- Poor self-esteem
- Anxiety and feeling overwhelmed

Stress shows up in two primary ways: as chronic or acute but short-lived stress. Research suggests short-lived, high-level stress may actually be good for helping your brain produce new neurons. Neurons affect a part of the brain responsible for improving memory and mental performance.

On the other hand, chronic stress for extended periods of time can put you at risk of developing a multitude of health problems. It suppresses new nerve cell growth and inhibits memory. Recent findings also indicate that persistent stress can cause irreversible harm to the body's organs and major systems, including the digestive system, nervous system, reproductive system, respiratory system, cardiovascular system, immune system, and musculoskeletal system.

While all of this might seem alarming, keeping chronic stress at bay is possible and you should feel motivated to work toward a solution! Of course, feeling negative more often than not increases your stress levels. By adopting some of the techniques in this book, you and your family can implement more positive, stress-busting habits.

Stress-Reduction RX

There's no quick-fix approach to minimizing stress, but stress recovery is possible. It begins with awareness. Just by reading this book, you have set your intention to awareness. The more "aha!" moments you notice as you travel on this journey, the more success you'll have in reducing your stress responses. (Try it, take a deep breath in and exhale with a loud "aha!" and you will release stress.) Don't worry! It takes time to develop that skill. However, if your plate is chock-full and you don't see any immediate way of changing that, it's most important to strive for balance. The deep diaphragmatic breathing, visualizations, affirmations, and muscle relaxation techniques you'll explore later in this book are proven antidotes for stress, but here are some other tools you can use throughout a busy day to help minimize the effects of chronic stress. These include:

- Exercise—moving your body daily helps you burn off steam, while instilling a healthy habit that not only helps mitigate stress, but also benefits your brain, heart—and waistline.
- Reframes—repositioning a seemingly negative occurrence in a more positive light may not come naturally to you, but with a little practice, you'll be able to find the silver lining in any situation, and this glass-half-full mentality is a great stress buffer.
- Simplifying—getting rid of all that no longer serves you (whether it's physical objects or obligations you dread) can help minimize the feeling of clutter in your life and contribute to a more peaceful existence.
- Scheduled downtime—a mentor once called this "hammock time"! Giving yourself permission to laze about for half an hour a day can be one of the best gifts you can give your overworked nervous system.
- Developing an attitude of gratitude—it is impossible to feel stress and gratitude in the same moment, so cultivating a daily practice of expressing gratitude for all that you have can go a long way towards reclaiming your happiness.

Handling Work Stress

The constant juggling act between work and home can take a toll on your personal health, and chip away at your family unity. Stress depletes your mental and physical energy—key elements needed to maintain a productive work level and cohesive family. Relaxation revives and rejuvenates, empowering you to face your duties with clarity and enthusiasm. While completely unplugging during the workday is not an option for most of us, there are small steps you can take during the day to nurture yourself. Try listening to relaxing music, focusing on your breathing, reading an inspirational passage, or allowing yourself to drift away on a happy thought for a few minutes.

More tricks of the trade include:

1. **Get Out of the Kitchen.** If you are a WAHM (work-at-home mom) or corporate mom, meet other working moms for lunch or attend networking events. By speaking with others, you get out of your own head and gain valuable insight. You might realize that your professional achievements are even more impressive than you thought.

2. **Surround Yourself with Dream Keepers.** Spend your time and share your ideas with friends and relatives who believe in you. A positive attitude supported by positive people will help manifest positive results.

3. **Outsource.** Realize you cannot be an expert in every area. Hire help on an as-needed basis, or consider what tasks you can delegate at work. Even one hour a week of offloading or outsourcing can free up precious time you can use to revitalize your soul.

4. **Be Prepared.** When you have an important deadline or task at work, carve the necessary time out of your day to be prepared. Passion coupled with preparedness reduces worries and pays off at work—and at home.

5. **Dress for Success.** Whether you are a WAHM or SAHM (stay-at-home mom), save the pajamas for a mental health/wellness day by yourself or with your family. When you look successful and pulled together, you will feel more positive and upbeat. Dress for success or plain old happiness. Colors can chase the doldrums away. Even a simple change of color in your wardrobe can improve your outlook for the day.

6. **Speak from Your Heart.** When you speak from your heart, people listen. When you are truly heard, miscommunication is far less likely to occur—decreasing the potential for the stress caused by misunderstandings or untruths.

7. **Visualize.** Use the power of visualization for both career success and work-life balance. Close your eyes, take a deep breath, and imagine what it would feel like to receive the job offer of your dreams, or picture yourself leaving your job for the day satisfied with the work you've completed and ready to enjoy the rest of your day with your family.

8. **Rally Your Family.** Involve your children. Let them share and participate in your professional aspirations, whether that's listening to you practice for a presentation or helping you select an outfit for your first day at a new job. Share the stress antidote of hope and enthusiasm.

MINDFUL MANTRA

Just for today, I know that I have done everything
I can possibly do for this day.

STRESS-LESS ACTIVITY: TAKE TIME OUT FOR YOU

Arrange for your husband or friend to take the kids to a movie or an activity that leaves you alone in your own space, house, or apartment for a couple of hours. Instead of doing laundry, working, or running out to do errands, enjoy staying in your own space and do something for you. Take a luxurious bath using lavender infused bath salts or decadent Dead Sea bath salts. Treat yourself to a bubble bath instead of your usual shower and nurture your inner child. Surround yourself with candles and take your time knowing the kids won't be yelling "Mom!" Enjoy the quiet or crank up tunes from your high school days. Believe that you are worth it.

Schedule 20–30 minutes of downtime each day so both you and your kids can take a break from each other and recharge. This doesn't have to equate to "nap time," but carving out time to wind down is an effective way to diffuse stress and overstimulation:

- Go to the library for some peace and quiet.
- Shut off your cell phone for a few hours or an entire day.
- Take yourself out to lunch at a non-kid-friendly restaurant.
- Enjoy a movie at the movie theater sans kids.
- Go for a bike ride with just your thoughts.
- Sign up for an art class or pursue a hobby you always dreamed of.
- Take a nap and don't feel guilty about it.
- Catch up on phone calls when you can't be interrupted.
- Spend time outside listening to the sounds of nature. Be sure to look up as the very act of looking up can lift your mood.

Parent's POV
On Introducing Mindfulness to Kids

"I am a disabled vet who suffers from chronic severe pain. Among the non-drug treatments I use are meditation and mindfulness to help me get through the breakthrough pain. My daughter saw me meditating one evening and wanted to know more about it (which thrilled me). I saw this as an opportunity to introduce her to some useful life tools. She loves guided visualization and positive affirmations, and she asks me to listen to one of them with her each night at bedtime. She is enjoying this first step and is ready for more!" —John

Monkey See, Monkey Do

As touched on earlier, an anxious family member affects the entire family. If you demonstrate healthy ways to manage and reduce anxiety your children will follow. Schedule downtime, watch what your children are being exposed to on TV, and give them boundaries. Handle situations with composure and give your children the tools to counteract stress, anger, and anxiety. Your children can become active participants in creating their own peaceful, calm, healthy lives. By demonstrating self-care, self-love, and self-respect, you become a healthy model for your children. Focus on integrating relaxation and stress management into your family's life. Be the calm you wish your children to be.

❦

MINDFUL MANTRA

Just for today, I am honoring my need for quiet time.

ⅭⅩ LORI'S LESSON ⅩⅭ

Each day brings numerous opportunities for you to incorporate stress management and healthy solutions. Breathing can be done almost anywhere, anytime. Focus on breathing when you are standing on line, taking a walk, going to bed, or even while you are sitting in the car for school pickups. When you practice breathing at home, invite your child to sit beside you or climb onto your lap. You can place your infant on your belly or hold her close to your chest so that she can feel your breathing. A toddler can put her hands on your belly to feel your belly go up and down. If breathing is your go-to tool, it will become your child's. Demonstrating is always the most powerful teaching tool. If something feels good to a child she's more likely to want to experience it again.

Stress: The New Norm

Although they might not have the words to express this, children want happy parents who aren't stressed-out. Studies show that kids know when their parents are stressed-out and it makes them feel sad. Kids are most happy when they feel like their parents are balanced and happy with life.

But these days the overall message children receive is that *everybody's* stressed-out, especially their parents. And this is normal. The next message they take in is how you handle stress. Do you turn to anger, binge eating, or drinking? Do you become angry and fly off the handle? Do you shut down and feel depressed? If so, it's important to become aware of your habits and get help in overcoming them so that you can show your children a healthy alternative. As parents, it's your responsibility to expose your children to coping skills they can use throughout their lives.

For example, in lieu of turning to reality TV to zone out when the stress becomes too hard to handle, you could instead rely on your newly acquired stress-reduction techniques. Imagine the effect on your child if you model this behavior by saying, "I'm stressed. I'm going to sit down and breathe deeply." Or, instead of having a short fuse during a homework session (as a result of chronic stress), you say, "I don't remember how to do this math, but let's figure it out together." Modeling behavior and demonstrating to your children ways in which they can show up in the world without succumbing to stress equips them with invaluable tools to cope. You can learn to respond instead of reacting. Taking a deep breath allows this response to develop.

If children learn to manage stress, they are better off later on in life. Case in point: Studies show children who practice relaxation techniques experience fewer visits to the doctor's office.

Children copy what they see and feel. Stress, anxiety, and anger are easily mimicked. It's very common for parents to unknowingly contribute to their child's stress. One stressed-out family member can increase the stress levels for the whole family. Anxious parents usually have anxious children. Mean parents usually have mean children and on it goes. But the good news is that one calm family member can affect the family in the same way.

You are in such a great position to model using relaxation techniques to counteract stress. You will learn many of these techniques as you work through this book, but it boils down to this:

- Demonstrate self-care, self-love, and self-respect.
- Focus on integrating relaxation and stress management into your family's life.

- Avoid overscheduling.
- Use self-esteem-building statements in regard to yourself and your children.
- Trust your parenting intuition.
- Surround yourself with dream keepers (people who support your dreams).
- Participate in healthy relationships.
- And most important: Lead by example.

SANITY SAVER   You can't always make things perfect. Constantly rethinking the past and critiquing how you could have, should have, or would have done it differently causes guilt and stress. If your "should"ers ache, it could be from using these words. Make imperfect your new perfect.

Parent's POV
On Overparenting
"I think I may suffer from this! I think time for yourself is important when parenting in general as well as not expecting too much of yourself. Easier said than done!" —Naomi

Shift Overparenting to Soulful Parenting

Overparenting, also called helicopter parenting, can cause undue stress. This usually comes from a place of fear. You may be afraid your children will get their feelings hurt, or make a less-than-perfect choice, or bump their knees. Parents often worry about their child falling "on their watch," which can result in treating their child as if he needs to be in bubble wrap. Fear-based parenting creates anxiety for parents and children. The perfectionist, type-A personalities of some working moms have the potential to translate into helicopter parenting at home.

This makes sense when you consider that moms in the workforce prior to having kids had to be persistent, aggressive, and in control at their jobs. It's common to transfer that approach to being a parent.

When you relax, you can begin to parent from a place of calm and knowing. You gain access to a parenting soul that allows you to trust yourself, your knowledge, and your ability to parent. You begin to realize that childhood is filled with bumps and bruises. You see these as teaching moments when your children gain access to the coping skills they will need for the rest of their lives. By overprotecting your children you rob them of experiences that shape them. When you wrap them in bubble wrap and refuse to let go of the back of their bike you send them the message that you don't believe in them. But when you let go and watch them right their wheels, you let your children know that they are capable. *When my daughter rode her bike alone for the first time, she exclaimed . . . "I think I am dreaming . . ."*

> *Imagine . . .*
> Close your eyes, take a deep breath, and imagine your child accomplishing a new milestone. See how this contributes to her self-value and lets her know that she is capable.

What if you could shift from a parenting position of needing to control the outcome so that it's perfect to parenting with soul? Parenting from your soul evokes feelings of truth, hope, and love. Parenting from a soulful place reduces stress, anxiety, and fear.

Author, educator, and parent Annie Burnside, MEd, specializes in this area, and here she shares ten ways to embrace soulful parenting:

1. Utilize everyday life—such as friendships, nature, mealtimes, music, movies, and much more—as the perfect curriculum and forum to teach your children powerful, universal principles such as connectedness, self-love, presence, and forgiveness.

2. Teach your children to allow multiple perspectives in all life situations and relationships by "flipping" challenges into positive learning opportunities.

3. Train your children to be more conscious of thoughts, words, and deeds so that they can assume greater responsibility for the shaping of their own reality.

4. Encourage compassion, empathy, and gratitude in your children on a daily basis by making them the most-used words in your home.

5. Turn the JOY in family life way up by singing, dancing, smiling, humming, laughing, and relaxing rigid perspectives as often as possible through openness and gratitude.

6. Model authenticity through speaking and living your truth, thereby giving your children permission to do the same.

7. Show your spirit daily so that your children can witness multiple aspects of you, and in turn, see multiple aspects in *themselves.*

8. Teach your children that they are intuitive, creative beings—and filled with infinite possibility.

9. Assist your children in understanding that an appreciation for life in the present moment, coupled with enthusiasm for their future, plants the necessary seeds for manifesting their true heart's desires.

10. Provide the space and opportunity for your children to focus on their interior world as much as the exterior world, allowing greater intimacy with the voice of their own soul to feel what resonates as truth for *them.*

SANITY SAVER   When you parent from your soul, you reserve the right to change your mind. A parenting choice that served you yesterday, may not serve you today.

Here's an example of soulful parenting in action: If your toddler is on the playground and you see a struggle about to occur with another kid over a toy, check your urge to jump in by taking a moment to breathe and observe. Your child might throw a tantrum—but she might also deal with the problem positively in her own way. If you pause, you might get to see the things you've been trying to teach her. When you pause, you allow space for beauty, wisdom, and transformation. The pause is a stress-management tool that allows magic to enter your life. What a joyful moment for you to see your child handle her own situation—and what a pivotal moment for your child! *(My parenting soul sings when I hear or see my children teach their friends something they learned from me. One such moment was when my young daughter suggested to her friend that she try taking some Vitamin C for her cough. My heart still smiles even years later.)*

⚜

MINDFUL MANTRA

Just for today, I will parent from my soul and
trust my parenting intuition.

CHAPTER 2

Identifying Your Child's Stress

"Parents need to teach their kids to balance human doing with human being."

—PAULA BLOOM

ℭ⛥ LORI'S LESSON ℘☊

Adults often forget to see things from a child's perspective. I knew a child who heard her dad might get fired. As a teen she recalled that for months she was fearful that her dad was going to catch on fire. You can alleviate so much fear by discussing the situation at hand with your children, and providing a reasonable outcome. Little ones do not understand adult situations and should be reminded that above all they are safe and loved. Here's one way to handle it: "Daddy might get fired which means he might lose his job. If dad were to lose his job we will do A, B, and C—and we will be fine. Just remember that we love you no matter what happens!"

As parents, your gut instinct goes a long way towards discerning how stress is affecting your child. Here you'll learn how to recognize how stress manifests for your child.

—- Relax FAQ —-

Q: What are some signs of stress in children? How do I identify stress in my kids?

A: Some signs to look out for are clingy behavior, nightmares, bedwetting, stomachaches, headaches; and all kinds of aches or pains that don't seem to have any validity. Preoccupation with a particular incident, teeth grinding, frequent meltdowns, withdrawing from friends and family, and changes in sleeping patterns are additional signs. All that said, it is really difficult to identify stress in children because a lot of these things are also normal for kids, too. So, ultimately, it's mostly about a more distinct CHANGE in behavior in which you notice a big shift. It's also really about INSTINCT. Parents know what's going on before anybody else does. So if something in the back of your head is saying, "Something's going on with my kid," don't push that thought away. Pull it to the front and pay attention to it. Trust yourself. You are your child's greatest advocate.

> *Imagine . . .*
> Close your eyes, take a deep breath, and imagine trusting your parenting intuition as you relax into knowing this is a powerful tool only you can access.

Children do not think, act, or manage stress like adults; the younger the child the smaller the stressors. Arriving at school to find a rearranged classroom or a substitute teacher can be big stressors to kids. Young children do not have the ability to identify or express their feelings of stress, making it important for teachers and parents to observe changes in behavior.

Sound Familiar?

Your child is having a meltdown in the middle of the department store. She's wailing for no apparent reason. She is refusing to move and is kicking at merchandise. She is angry with her brother and has announced that she isn't going to move from that spot. How do you handle this scenario? Do you threaten to punish her when you get home? Do you secretly wonder if you're a bad parent? Do you bribe her with a toy, or do you decide she is just having a bad day . . . again?

MINDFUL MANTRA

Just for today, I will meet my child's tantrum
with love and calm. I know that the reward for
love filled parenting—is love filled parenting.

Your automatic conclusion is likely that your child is merely being difficult or seeking attention. Or perhaps you see this as a sign that she's coming down with a cold or just tired. But here's the thing: Your child is most likely feeling the effects of stress. If an adult friend lashed out in a similar fashion, would you assume the same, or would you understand on some level that they were reacting to their hectic, demanding lifestyle? If your friend acted out in this way, you may suggest a yoga class or relaxation retreat, but little ones do not have the luxury of scheduling these kinds of stress-reducing activities. In fact, without proper education around it, kids don't even understand the phrase "stressed-out" to explain how they feel. You may have given them language to express what a headache or stomachache feels like. Likewise, you've helped them convey when they are hungry. But have you taught them how to identify when they are feeling stressed-out and how to express that they need some downtime?

SANITY SAVER   Give kids words for feelings. Words are an outlet for children; they help reduce frustration and give you better insight about what's really going on inside their world.

What Traumatic Stress Looks Like

As we touched on in Chapter 1, there's a difference between acute stress and chronic stress. But stress can sometimes take a turn for the worse, especially when it's precipitated by a traumatic event such as a natural disaster or a national tragedy. Studies show that children who have experienced such an event may display signs of being agitated, overactive, confused, afraid, angry, sad, anxious, or withdrawn. Keep a close eye on your child during these periods and watch for these symptoms. A key warning sign may be your little one's preoccupation with the traumatic event, his or her pulling back from family and friends, experiencing disturbed sleep, or physical complaints for no apparent reason. These may indicate stress or even Post-Traumatic Stress Disorder (PTSD). PTSD is characterized by the delayed onset of stress after exposure to something traumatic. This delayed reaction has the potential to linger for years. While commonly associated with the soldiers who suffer from it, PTSD also affects children. According to studies, every year upwards of 3,000,000 children show signs of this intense and sometimes debilitating form of stress.

Millions of children have been affected by traumatic events such as the Newtown, Connecticut school shooting, the Boston Marathon bombing, and the use of chemical weapons in Syria. The average household has the television turned on for seven hours a day which means children are exposed to unprecedented images of trauma. These scenes can be difficult for most adults to manage, so you can only imagine how it affects children. Kids lack the emotional tools to make sense of tragic events and the coping skills needed to maintain some state of normalcy in the face of extreme events. Unlike adults, children often believe that a traumatic event is happening over and over again, which exacerbates the stress they feel. For example, when the media kept showing the planes hitting the Twin Towers on 9/11, adults realized this was the same scene being replayed, but many children believed more and more buildings were being hit. It's important to realize that kids who have experienced a catastrophic event, whether directly or indirectly, can be candidates for emotional distress or Post-Traumatic Stress Disorder.

Choosing a Therapist for Your Child's Anxiety

If your child displays any of the warning signs of anxiety (or stress that has become debilitating), you need to get him or her professional care from a qualified therapist. During a consultation, the therapist should be willing to answer any questions you may have about methods, training, and fees. Be prepared to discuss your child's symptoms in detail, and be sure to share any medications for allergies or other illnesses your child currently takes.

Here are some questions to consider asking (courtesy of the Anxiety and Depression Association of America (ADAA)).

- What training and experience do you have in treating child anxiety disorders?
- Do you specialize in treating children? (If your child is a teenager, you may want to ask the age limit that your child can remain under this specialist's care.)
- What is your training in cognitive-behavioral therapy (CBT) or other therapies?
- What is your basic approach to treatment?
- Can you prescribe medication or refer me to someone who can, if that proves necessary?
- How long is the course of treatment?
- How frequent are treatment sessions and how long do they last?
- Do you include family members in therapy?
- How will I know that my child is responding to the treatment and getting better?
- If my child does not respond to treatment, how will you decide when to change or modify the treatment?
- As my child ages, will any symptoms change? Will the response to treatment change?
- What should I explain to the school about my child's anxiety disorder?
- How do you approach the topic of alcohol and substance use in teens who take medication?
- Will you coordinate my child's treatment with our family doctor or pediatrician?
- What is your fee schedule, and do you have a sliding scale for varying financial circumstances?
- What kinds of health insurance do you accept?

You'll also want to discuss relaxation techniques with your therapist. A therapist who offers a mix of holistic and traditional modalities may offer the best treatment for your child. If a therapist is reluctant to answer your questions, or if you or your child does not feel comfortable, ask a trusted friend or health care professional for a referral to a new therapist!

How Stressed Is Your Child?

The American Psychological Association (APA) released results from a survey that reveal that parents are out of touch when it concerns their kids' stress levels. In fact, one in eight children experience some kind of anxiety disorder and many more are just stressed-out! The APA reports the greatest stress sources for kids are related to school pressure and family finances, and that parents often underestimate how stressed their kids really are. Children's Hospital Boston psychiatrist Stuart Goldman, MD, weighed in about how you can help manage your children's stress and how you can be more in sync with what's bothering your kids.

Q: Why aren't parents more perceptive to their child's feelings of stress?

A: Teens and tweens are known for being inexplicably moody or irritable. When a child does the stereotypical stomping up the stairs accompanied by a loud, "Leave me alone!" it's often perceived as moodiness, when in fact it could actually be a sign of stress, anxiety, or depression. From a psychiatric point of view, parents underappreciate how a child internalizes problems (anxiety or depression), in contrast to when the child external izes problems (misbehavior).

Q: What signs indicate a heightened level of stress in a child?

A: Be aware of changes in a child's behavior, such as aggressiveness, acting much younger than she is, or no longer enjoying the things she used to. Irritableness, headaches, stomachaches, and fatigue are also signs of stress. These symptoms indicate ❯❯

that something of significance may be going on, and if they go unnoticed, they may progress into more serious problems.

Q: What are the long-term health implications of stress?

A: With a longer-term stress disorder, sadness can turn into depression and worries may turn into an anxiety disorder. It's also thought by many that stress can compromise general health or immune functioning, resulting in less resistance to disease.

Q: What can parents do to be more in tune with their children's stress?

A: As children grow older, they are constantly seeking more independence. The idea of them requesting help from their parents flies in the face of the greater autonomy they seek. Parents must be sensitive to the subtle or not-so-subtle behavior of their kids and know to be concerned if the degree of change is great. Take notice of the difference in your child's behavior when she is in school as opposed to when she is on vacation. This is a great way to assess if school pressure is adding stress to your child's life.

Q: How can parents keep their own stress from affecting their kids?

A: Children need to be realistically included in the difficulties a family is facing. Parents need to reassure their children the best they can and need to know when kids should be insulated to a certain degree. Parents have the idea that if they don't talk about their problems (marital problems, finances), their kids won't know about them. The reality is that kids invariably know much earlier on about these problems than parents think they do.

SANITY SAVER Remember that children are beginners (not just yours), so be patient with them.

A Stressed Kid Often Looks Like This

A stressed-out child may be jumpy, asking lots of questions and worried about upcoming events that would not normally cause them concern. She may overhear radio and TV news events and become preoccupied with what she heard. A stressed-out child may be aware of terrorist attacks and school shootings—and she may talk about it more than her siblings or peers. Does this merely mean she's being exposed to too much too soon, and the symptoms of stress are showing? Or is she becoming the nervous type?

Consider another scenario: Your usually happy, enthusiastic child seems extremely blue. He is quiet, withdrawn, and isn't interested in playing with his best friend. His energy level is low and he says that nothing is hurting or bothering him. Is this a phase or something more serious?

Or, perhaps your child seems tired. He is sleepy during the day and has been having trouble quieting his mind at bedtime. During the night he has started having nightmares and wakes up frequently. What could be the cause—an uncomfortable bed, a reaction to something in his diet, or stress?

Different Stress for Different Folks

Stress shows up differently for each individual and can be difficult to detect. Many of the indicators are emotions and behaviors children exhibit on a regular basis. There are variables to consider such as age, family stability, and coping skills. The arrival of a new teacher midyear might create anguish and stress for a 5-year-old whereas a 13-year-old might actually *welcome* the change. Remember: Stress is not an isolated event that happens to us; stress is a REACTION to an event. Stress is an accepted way of life in today's society.

Types of Stress

The National Scientific Council on the Developing Child has identified three main types of stress:

1. **Positive stress**—results from adverse experiences that are short-lived. Children may encounter positive stress when they attend a new daycare, meet new people, or have a toy taken away from them. This type of stress causes minor physiological changes including an increase in heart rate and changes in hormone levels. With the support of caring adults, children can learn how to manage and overcome positive stress. This type of stress is considered normal and coping with it is an important part of the development process.

2. **Tolerable stress**—refers to adverse experiences that are more intense but still relatively short-lived. Examples include the death of a loved one, a natural disaster, a frightening accident, and family disruptions such as separation or divorce. If a child has the support of a caring adult, tolerable stress can usually be overcome. In many cases, tolerable stress can become positive stress and benefit the child developmentally. However, if the child lacks adequate support, tolerable stress can become toxic and lead to long-term negative health effects.

3. **Toxic stress**—results from intense adverse experiences that may be sustained over a long period of time—weeks, months, or even years. An example of toxic stress is child maltreatment, which includes abuse and neglect. Children are unable to effectively manage this type of stress by themselves. As a result, the stress response system gets activated for a prolonged amount of time. This can lead to permanent changes in the development of the brain. The negative effects of toxic stress can be lessened with the support of

caring adults. Appropriate support and intervention can help in returning the stress response system back to its normal baseline.

Researchers have studied and documented the effects of stress on our brains and bodies. From the monitoring of blood lactate levels to the easily measured heart and respiratory rates, the scientific community has proven that stress, although intangible, is powerful and harmful to humans. Stress is front and center, and many doctors consider it to be a silent killer.

Your Instinct Counts!

Recognizing stress in newborns, toddlers, and children is difficult. Babies might stiffen their bodies, arch their backs, grimace, and cry for any number of reasons. Your parent-child connection strengthens as you learn to recognize your infant's needs. You begin to rely on and realize that you need to *trust your instincts*. Toddlers might display a change in eating and sleeping habits or become more aggressive. It is often difficult to discern if these are normal developmental stages or signs of stress. At all stages, parents, especially moms, know when something is out of sync with their children. Keep an eye out for a change in your child's behavior. For example: clingy behavior is a sign of stress in toddlers. However, some toddlers are clingy. So if your child is usually not the clingy type and she's suddenly attached to your leg, then that would be considered a change in behavior.

Some of the signs in children also include: no longer wanting to go to school, an increase in nightmares or night terrors, and difficulty falling and staying asleep. Physical symptoms can present themselves as unexplained stomachaches, headaches, bedwetting, and starting new self-soothing habits like thumb sucking and hair twirling. Sometimes the child will withdraw from friends and family members, or have frequent meltdowns, which is a common sign of stress for toddlers. As discussed in Chapter 1, it's important for you to learn to manage your own stress because all children (from babies to teens) pick up on it. You can instead choose to set a stress-less example and cultivate calm.

STRESS-LESS ACTIVITY: TUNE IN TO YOUR INNER PARENTING

For one week, dedicate five minutes each day to listen to your inner voice—a.k.a. your gut or intuition. Sit quietly. Close your eyes. Take a deep breath, and as you do, breathe in the words "calm parenting" and on your exhale, breathe out the words "calm parenting." By calming yourself in this way you will be better positioned to access your inner parent.

MINDFUL MANTRA

Just for today, I honor my inner parenting voice. It guides me and gives me valuable insight into my child's well-being.

The bottom line? A relaxed parent makes better decisions. You are faced with decisions regarding your children every day. Some are life changing. Stress gets in the way of clear thinking. When you take the time to quiet your mind you clear out the stress static long enough to access answers. It bears repeating: Relaxed parents make better decisions.

CHAPTER 3

Kids Don't Come with Directions, but *Need* Direction

> *"The child supplies the power but the parents have to do the steering."*
> —DR. BENJAMIN SPOCK

ℰ⤖ LORI'S LESSON ⤕ℐ

*I have children visit my house that come from families with fewer bound-
aries and some of them have high anxiety. When I set boundaries (or rules
if you want to call them that), within minutes of them operating in my
home I can see their stress levels dropping. It's because kids want to know
what's right and wrong. They want to know how far in the street they can
or can't go. Children feel safer when they know that the adult in their life
is invested enough to show them that they need to stay on the curb. Their
life is calmer if it's not left up to them to make choices about where the
boundaries are or what the rules are. It really is a parent's job with young
children and it sets a good foundation from which a child can grow into a
teen and adult that can set healthy boundaries for themselves. And it does
produce secure, happy children.*

Love

Love is the glue that holds the family together so you'll want to show
your affection for your children in many varied ways. It is impossible
for the pure, light feeling of love and the dense, foggy feeling of stress
to exist at the same moment. If you can tap into the feeling of love,
you will reduce stress. Children want you to love yourself enough to
express your true self. Do not lose the essence of you; otherwise, you
deny your children your beauty. Speaking of beauty, also tell your
children they are beautiful . . . no matter how young or old they are.

Other ways to demonstrate love for your kids include:

- Speaking their language by keeping up with technology.
- Learning to text.
- Telling them you like their friends.
- Sending them photos of your pets.
- Putting little love notes in their pockets, on a bathroom mirror,
  on their pillows, or in their lunch boxes.
- Giving extra hugs.

- Laughing and having fun with them.
- Focusing on breathing before you greet them.
- Unplugging and being fully present when they speak to you.

> *Imagine . . .*
> Close your eyes, take a deep breath, and imagine what it feels like to give and receive unconditional love. Breathe in love, and out love . . .

With your children, tweens, and teens, also make sure to tell them that you like (LIKE) them! It has a distinctly different energy as your kids assume you LOVE them, but when you let them know you *like* them, it's as if you are seeing them for who they really are. In order to accomplish this, you must be in the position of an observer. You can take deep breaths, pause and note to yourself that you are observing. This very moment of creating observer awareness will allow you to see aspects of you and your child you never noticed before.

MINDFUL MANTRA
Just for today, I will choose loving and kind words
when I speak to my child. I know that one day
these words will become her inner voice.

Balance

For many of you, the concept of balance may feel like an elusive dream—something that's always just out of reach. But don't give up on the notion because it doesn't seem achievable. Small steps taken towards minimizing stress levels over a long period of time can indeed bring about significant changes in your lifestyle. Remember: It's all about your choices in the NOW and it's about persistence, not perfection. When you make decisions with a keen eye towards not tipping the scales in any one direction, you will get closer to an equilibrium that brings your family into balance.

Signs of Imbalance

One way to know if your life is out of balance (or to measure your life balance), is to notice how many times a week you eat fast food. Fast food means fast life. Often when we are out of balance we have physical aches and pains. Is your body sending you a message of pain to try to get you to slow down? Are you or your children getting sick a lot? Stress sends the immune system into a state of imbalance making it harder to resist illness. Are you resentful of your life? Do you feel like you're living out of your car? Are you chronically fatigued? All of these signs of imbalance are nothing to fret about. Take a step back, be an observer of how you feel and how you are living your life. Ask yourself how you can make a change to restore balance. Keep in mind: Most meltdowns for young children are due to being tired or hungry. Don't ask too much of your children. They have simple needs that they want met. Don't overschedule. If you do, you create stressed-out, angry children. Think about whether busy is good. Society says busy is good, but it's time to reevaluate that. Children need balance and downtime. So do adults!

ᐉᕁ LORI'S LESSON ᕦᕁ

So many parents have been taught to get busy when dealing with difficult emotions that inevitably come up when you experience life on life's terms. Adults do this to avoid facing unpleasant emotions, thus internalizing the belief that being busy equates to being happy. Often we project this idea onto our children and get them overly busy so that we can sit back and pat ourselves on the backs for making our children happy. Do not confuse busy with happy. A busy child is not necessarily a HAPPY child.

MINDFUL MANTRA
Just for today, I will slow down and
experience the joy of doing nothing.

What Does Exercise Have to Do with It?

How many times do you tell your kids to stop jumping on the bed or jumping around the house? Well, jumping stimulates the lymphatic system, which boosts our immune system. Even babies jump when you stand them on your lap. Are they jumping for joy? Or are they tapping into innate wisdom to participate in keeping themselves healthy? Jumping usually leads to laughter, which is a double dose of wellness! Laughter is a proven stress reducer and immune system enhancer.

When kids are exposed to regular physical activity they are more likely to carry these healthy habits into their adult lives. Getting outside, running, jumping, playing sports, and burning off excess energy all contribute to the production of feel-good brain chemicals that help ward off the negative health toll that stress takes on the body.

Again, just as children pick up on your stress and model your behavior, so will they with exercise. If you model good, healthy, active habits and plan family outings such as hiking, swimming, or biking, or even jumping and laughing, you succeed in giving your children an invaluable gift that they will carry into adulthood.

What Does Diet Have to Do with It?

Stress-reducing foods can be an important ingredient in your family's overall wellness plan. The right foods can reduce stress, anxiety, and fatigue. When you expose children to more than the "children's menu," you introduce them to a variety of healthy foods they are more likely to taste and like.

ℰ𝒮 LORI'S LESSON 𝒮ℰ

Parents are amazed to hear that their child ate artichokes, salmon, and quinoa at my house. Kids are more likely to eat a healthy food when they help to prepare it, grow it, or assign a fun name to it. Quinoa is an amazing seed that can be incorporated into your family's diet. I put it in a soup with chopped carrots, broccoli, and red potatoes. The kids refused to taste it until we named it Halloween soup because of its orange color. Now we eat Halloween soup at my house all year round!

With children, it's important to make sure they are eating healthy meals and snacks at regular intervals throughout the day, while not snacking excessively (this can throw off their hunger signals and make them less apt to eat their meals). A consistent schedule for eating helps keep your little ones' blood sugar stable and can help ward off tantrums and mood swings. It is easy to overlook your child's eating schedule when you are distracted by activities, but here's the thing: By the time young children communicate to you that they are hungry, they are usually already getting cranky. Children like to eat smaller, more frequent meals, which contributes to their overall emotional and physical stability.

Eating meals and snacks that have a balanced amount of healthy whole carbohydrates, lean protein, and healthy fats (e.g., olive oil, coconut oil, avocado, nuts, and seeds) also helps contribute to stabilizing blood sugar and providing little bodies with the proper nutrition they need to grow and thrive.

When the body is not in balance nutritionally, sometimes the culprit can be underlying and undiagnosed food allergies. Food allergies can heighten stress in children and also may cause mood disturbances, so if you suspect your child may be experiencing a reaction after consuming certain foods, you should follow up with your medical doctor or holistic doctor to have him or her tested for allergies.

I have had much success with kinesiology, acupressure, and proper use of vitamins and minerals in treating food allergies. Vitamin C and essential fatty acids (EFAs) have anti-inflammatory properties and can help children in their battle with allergies. I believe in the barrel overload theory (see below) when combating allergies. Be relentless and seek out modalities that work for your family. Talk to other parents and share ideas, support, and experiences.

Another option is to put your child through a simple elimination diet in which you eliminate one category of food for fourteen days and then reintroduce it and watch for how your child reacts. If you're not sure where to start, notice what food your child craves on a continual basis. Start by eliminating that item as it has a high chance of being the cause of the trouble. Keep a food journal to see if you notice any patterns or correlation between foods consumed and change in behavior, stuffy noses, headaches, or sleep. Food and environmental allergies can affect not only your child's health, but also his behavior. (Dr. Doris Rapp's full barrel theory combined with Dr. Crook's wisdom on the yeast connections changed my life in this regard. If you notice that your child can go from collected to out of control in a minute, it may be worth looking into Dr. Rapp and Dr. Crook's theories. You may find that your child is overloaded—his barrel is overflowing. When you see it in this way, you realize you can help keep his barrel from overflowing by applying many of the techniques you are reading about in this book.)

You'll discover valuable affirmations you can use with your children to reinforce eating nourishing foods and staying active in the story *Caterpillar Choices* (*Indigo Dreams: Garden of Wellness*).

❦

MINDFUL MANTRA

Just for today, I will notice how I feel after I eat various foods. I will leave room in my barrel so that it can be filled with wellness.

ᴄ᷒ᴑ LORI'S LESSON ᴑ᷒

My son's food and environmental allergies wreaked havoc on his behavior and his ability to fall asleep and stay asleep. Many nights were disrupted by hives, stuffy nose, and coughing. Many days were riddled with hyperactivity and notes from teachers. We eliminated offending foods and used vitamins and minerals designed to soothe his nervous system. His behavior, health, and sleep patterns improved. My children are aware of how their food choices affect their overall health and well-being.

STRESS-LESS ACTIVITY: BUILD A HEALTHY FRUIT TREE

Children who eat a diet that's nutritionally balanced are better equipped to handle daily stressors. This fruit creation gets kids creating in the kitchen and eating lots of fiber-filled treats.

(Adapted from Live. Learn. Love. Eat. livelearnloveeat.com/?s=fruit+tree.)

- 1 pineapple
- 1 pear
- 2 cups strawberries, stems removed
- 6 ounces fresh raspberries
- 6 ounces fresh blackberries
- 2 kiwi, peeled and chopped
- 2 mandarin oranges, peeled and sectioned
- 1 cup red seedless grapes
- ½ cup chopped watermelon
- 1 large star-shaped cookie cutter
- 1 small heart-shaped cookie cutter (optional)
- at least 35 wooden toothpicks

1. Begin by cutting the top and bottom off of your pineapple. Save a 1-inch-thick slice of your pineapple as well for cutting the star out of. Cut all of the skin off of the outside of the pineapple so that only the edible portion remains. Slice the top of your pineapple as well to give it a slightly

pointed shape at the top. Save the edible pineapple scraps to decorate the tree with later.

2. Cut the bottom off of your pear and remove the stem. Use a toothpick to place the pear on top of the prepared pineapple. This is your tree.

3. Use the large star-shaped cookie cutter to cut out a star for the top of the tree from the reserved slice of pineapple.

4. Place the star on top of the tree with a wooden toothpick.

5. Insert many wooden toothpicks all over the pineapple and pear, fairly deep in so that they won't show once you have placed the fruit on them.

6. Decorate! Stick the prepared fruit onto the toothpicks all over the tree.

Guidance

As a parent, one of your main roles in your child's life is to provide guidance. Without guidance, your child doesn't receive the information he or she needs to successfully navigate the world. A child without guidelines or boundaries is a child with much stress.

Here are some of the many areas in which your children need your guidance:

- Handling social situations and friendships.
- Time management.
- Expressing how they feel, especially negative feelings.
- How to shake hands or introduce their friends to each other.
- Social skills—smiling and making eye contact.
- How to laugh at themselves and release hurt feelings.
- Developing a moral compass and compassion.
- How to be optimistic.

ℭ LORI'S LESSON ℧

I love teaching children to share in their friends' accomplishments and feel joy for them instead of jealousy. When children get in the habit of celebrating each other's accomplishments, we are setting them up for a lifetime of collaboration instead of competition. They become that person that adds value to the group and community.

While it may be tempting to buffer your children from disappointment, it's actually valuable to allow them to experience it. Teach them to move through it. For example, don't let your daughter win EVERY time you play a board game or cards. Don't call the school if your son gets a grade you don't agree with or a teacher he didn't want. The urge to protect your children from discouragement or setbacks is based in fear. What's more: If you send your children the message that the world revolves around them and their every need must be met or they won't be happy, they're more likely to grow up turning every less-than-perfect moment into a stressful situation. Instead, honor their feelings and teach them that the world will not always accommodate their every wish and desire. Your children need to develop resilience and flexibility.

MINDFUL MANTRA
Just for today, I will be flexible and I will allow my children to experience the ebbs and flows of life.

Doing too much for your children sends them a negative message that you do not believe they are capable and you do not believe in them. Empowering your children reduces stress and enables them to develop a sense of independence that will serve them later in life.

SANITY SAVER   Stress-Free Negotiating: Give your child a choice, but be sure that both choices lead to an outcome you desire. Nothing is worse than giving a child a choice you are hoping they don't pick.

Parent's POV
On Giving Your Child Choice

"I found this advice a win-win outcome when dealing with my young son's growing independence and me learning to let go and give in some. My son and I would argue about what I picked out for him to wear to school each day, so I decided to pick out three outfits the night before and let him choose the one he liked best and he went for it and was happy—plus, we had no more morning arguments about what he was going to wear." —Denice

Boundaries

Are you a "yes" parent? If so, you're not alone. This seems to be a byproduct of parents being too stressed, working too hard, and feeling guilty as a result. However, "no" is not a four-letter word—children need to hear the word "no" to be healthy! It's hard work to set boundaries for your children, but one that's essential to keep them from thinking the world revolves around them. Just think about how behavior on an airplane would improve if your kids were used to hearing "no" prior to the trip. Using the word "no" for the first time on the airplane will get you screams and resistance! You see, both you *and* your kids can benefit from setting clear boundaries and rules. You end up feeling less perturbed in the long run as your kids act up less when you make a simple request, and your little ones feel safer and calmer when they know where the boundaries are. Taking the time to say "no" is another way to show your children that you love and care about them.

Boundaries with Media

Be realistic about putting boundaries on media consumption in your home. You might want to implement an "unplug" rule to counteract the hours that the TVs are on, the laptops are open, and smartphones are buzzing. Putting a total moratorium on electronics usage is not only impractical; it's unlikely to get you anywhere. Instead, call a family meeting and get everyone's input on how to incorporate more face time and less screen time in your home. There are two benefits to this approach—by taking realistic steps to fix the problem, you are more likely to end up with a sustainable solution, and by getting family buy-in via a collective agreement, you are more likely to see your loved ones comply. Remember: You set the example here, so if you're just as guilty of spending too much time plugged in, you'll need to address that for yourself before you can expect your children to make a change.

Here are some tips for teaching your children how to navigate a complicated media landscape:

Close your eyes, turn away, and alert an adult. Teach children what to do if they encounter inappropriate images on the Internet. Pop-ups, spam e-mails, clicking unintended search results, or misspelled words are real threats in today's technology-driven world. Children are less fearful when they know how to handle being exposed to images that are frightening, unhealthy, or inappropriate. Children can close their eyes immediately, turn away from the computer, and alert an adult. Think of this as the "Stop, Drop, and Roll" of technology safety. According to a study at the University of New Hampshire's Crimes Against Children Research Center (CACRC), 42 percent of 10- to 17-year-olds reported they had been exposed to online pornography.

Rating systems are not parenting systems. Know what your children are watching and seeing online, on television, and in the movie theaters. Parents may not want their kids to see what appears to be a seemingly tame PG-13 movie, in which popular stars reference porn at least six times. While the mention of porn may not pose an immediate threat, it desensitizes your child or tween so that her internal warning flag many not go up when a friend suggests they look at some porn. Even G-rated family shows that you think are harmless musicals can surprise you. They may be singing about hooking up or attending a party where underage alcohol is glorified. These confusing messages may be a direct contrast to your family values. Televisions and computers are best left out of the bedrooms so you can keep an eye on their screens.

Inappropriate **and** *appropriate,* *healthy* **and** *unhealthy,* **are words to know and use.** The sooner your children understand these words, the easier it will be for you to discuss movies, TV, Internet, and sensitive issues. Fighting the statistics requires diligent parenting and honest conversations. Kids need to be taught what is appropriate or not (e.g., naked or partially nude photos are inappropriate). Even a 3-year-old can start to hear the word *inappropriate* and begin to understand its meaning.

Create a code with your child, tween, or teen. Kids are often pressured by their peers to watch a movie or TV show they are uncomfortable with or find to be terrifying. Be aware that many parents allow their children to watch or play video games with inappropriate amounts of violent and frightening material. This may not support your family's ideals and your child may not know how to get out of the situation. Remind your children to text or call you if they feel uncomfortable at anyone's home. Create a text code tweens can use to clue you in that they want you to call them and insist that you need them to come home. This allows them to get out of the situation and save face with their friends at the same time. Of course, you want your children to know how to stand up for themselves, but it is wise to also have a backup plan.

Discuss your rules with other parents. If your child is not allowed to watch violent movies or play violent video games, take a moment to let the other parent know your expectations when you drop her off for a playdate. Do not assume other families are as diligent as you are about media and video game exposure.

The American Pediatric Association says excessive TV viewing can contribute to poor grades, sleep problems, behavior problems, obesity, and risky behavior. TV bombards youth with confusing stressful messages about what the social norm is, and how to behave. The average child will watch 8,000 murders on TV before finishing elementary school. The media rewards and glamorizes bad behavior, inappropriate actions, and unhealthy choices. As parents, you need to counteract these damaging media messages with awareness and involvement. Children need a strong internal compass to navigate today's media-driven world.

—— Relax FAQ ——

Q: My daughter just turned 12 and is growing up so fast! I fear we will become disconnected, and it's becoming difficult for us to show her that we love her while also still enforcing our family boundaries. I find myself nagging more and more often. What do you recommend?

A: It is more important than ever to keep lines of communication open. One stress-free way to communicate with your tween is to write her a letter. Tweens have selective hearing and can check out the minute you ask them to put their clothes away. Below is an outline of a letter to a tween that can bring you closer and eliminate some stress and anger along the way.

> **Dear** _____:
> We are writing to you because Dad and I realize that you want to have freedom and do things without us nagging you, and we agree with you. We want to work together with you so that we can eliminate nagging and give you a plan to develop more independence. Please know that we support you and your quest to be more on your own. We want you to have a clear understanding of what is **>>**

expected of you and what your responsibilities are. This will help you achieve the independence you seek.

When you follow the suggestions on the list you will be rewarded with more privileges, independence, an allowance, and you will have a sense of accomplishment.

If you don't want to do what is on this list there will be consequences just like you have in school and will one day have in a job. If you don't complete something on time, such as homework/projects, chores, or if you act out, fail a test, you will lose privileges, your grades will drop, and bottom line you will lose trust, freedom, and independence.

[*Set the guidelines below in your own clear, succinct terms.*]

1.   Bedtime/Homework/Studies:
2.   Computer and Phone Use:
3.   Attitude/Honesty:
4.   Chores:
5.   Rewards:
6.   Consequences:

Please remember our door is ALWAYS open for you. We are your parents. We love you and respect you, and only want the same in return. We are always open to listen to your feelings/thoughts and even compromise on an issue we don't agree on. If we do this together, I know we will all be happier and it will help eliminate stress for all involved.

We love you,

Mom and Dad

This letter is meant as a springboard to your own letter. Expectations, rules, and times will vary from family to family. Use this as a guideline and personalize it, so that you can overcome resistance and create a solid foundation for your family.

Boundaries with Siblings

Clear boundaries mean less stress. It is never too early to teach children that healthy relationships have healthy boundaries. This applies to children, parents, friends—and especially siblings. It might seem easier to have a friend over for one of your children and force them to play with the other siblings. But kids need autonomy. Young children especially need time to learn how to develop one-on-one friendships so they can learn such concepts as sharing, cooperation, and taking turns. By creating a space for them to interact with their friends without interference from their siblings, you send a message to them that you value and honor their needs. You allow them to explore creating relationships that are separate from their family dynamics. Here are some simple guidelines to keep peaceful boundaries among siblings:

- Do not allow bullying behavior among siblings, name-calling, hitting, or constant put-downs.
- Do not force siblings to share friends.
- Spend quality time with each child separately.
- Teach siblings to respect each other's space, feelings, and things.
- Don't expect them to dress the same.
- Don't compare siblings to one another.
- Don't expect them to react to situations, circumstances, or discipline in the same way.
- When you treat your children as the individuals that they are, you model the respect upon which a foundation of good boundaries is built.

Parent's POV
On Setting Boundaries with Siblings

"My 6-year-old asked yesterday if I'd help him make a 'Do Not Disturb' sign for his bedroom door so his twin brothers (age 4) would know when to stay out. I thought it was great problem solving!" —Linda

Finally, realize that your children are individuals and they will be better equipped to handle teenage peer pressure and emerge as healthier, happier adults if they learn to develop a strong sense of boundaries early on. With the pillars of love, balance, guidance, and boundaries in place, you set the stage to equip your children with a reservoir of self-esteem and coping skills.

Arming your family with an arsenal of sincere compliments can make nurturing self-esteem a family affair.

STRESS-LESS ACTIVITY: PUT WORDS IN THEIR MOUTHS

Encourage kids to give each other more compliments. Get them started with this list.

- I like the way you help your friends.
- You are a good brother.
- I like the way you take turns.
- I like the way you share.
- I enjoy your company.
- You are kind.
- You are helpful.
- You are caring.
- I like the way you try your best.
- You are a good artist.
- You are a great sister.
- You are a good listener.

- You are very nice.
- I like when you sit with me at lunch.
- You are creative.
- I like the way you stick up for me.
- Your smile makes me smile.
- I like your laugh.
- You are polite.
- You have great ideas.
- You are fun.
- You are a terrific friend.

SANITY SAVER   Shift your thinking. "Nothing is impossible. The word itself says 'I'm possible.'" —Audrey Hepburn

CHAPTER 4

The Power of Play

> "Play is often talked about as if it were a relief from serious learning. But for children play is serious learning. Play is really the work of childhood."
>
> —FRED ROGERS

ℭ LORI'S LESSON ℘

When I think of happy, stress-free kids, I recall my own childhood filled with endless hours of unstructured playtime. Children of all ages playing together, laughing, and competing. I especially loved the dynamics of the older children teaching the younger children how to play Touch Football, Ringolevio, Chinese Jumprope, and Pickle in the Middle. Street games and tree climbing that went on and on, until our parents called us in. The lessons of collaboration, teamwork, exploration, and communication I learned during these moments still play a part in how I show up today.

Kids need the space to explore their world and need to be given an environment where they feel free to laugh, sing, play, make a mess, and be silly! Help your child by being flexible in this area. Don't be so concerned with the pillows being in the right place on the couch that you stop your children from using them to make a totem pole they end up dancing around. You might miss out on hours of free-flowing play that give you some entertainment and extra "me" time.

MINDFUL MANTRA

Just for today, I will let my inner child come out and play. My children will remember me as a mom who had time to play.

—— Staying Young at Heart ——

When was the last time you tried to do a headstand? Jumped into a pool or the ocean with your clothes on? Stopped your car to get out and pirouette under the falling leaves? Cuddled up under a blanket and watched the night sky for shooting stars?

These little things may not sound like much, but they're all examples of unbridled, childlike activities that can bring you great joy. You undoubtedly did these things, or at least thought about doing them, when you were a child—before the routine of adult life crept in.

A recent UCLA study showed just how different the creative life of a child is from that of an adult. Their study revealed that average 5-year-olds act creatively 98 times per day, laugh 113 times, and ask a whopping 65 questions per day. Compare that to the average 44-year-old, who participates in 2 creative activities, enjoys 11 laughs, and asks a mere 6 questions. Quite a difference!

While you are living your adult life, you can benefit from honoring the childlike energy within you. Consider these suggestions in order to reacquaint yourself with *your* inner child.

Dismantle your brick wall. Like many others, you may have your guard up or even have built an invisible brick wall around your heart. This wall is shielding out the good along with the bad. Maintaining this wall around your heart and soul is exhausting! It keeps you farther and farther removed from the ebbs and flows of a joyful life. Use your energy more efficiently by tearing down the bricks and embracing the up-and-down feelings of life.

Less work, more play! Release yourself from the stiff parameters of adulthood and goof off every once in awhile. Dance, sing, laugh, play, roll down a hill, jump in a leaf pile, and take delight in your children on a daily basis. You can create a space of willingness that lets playful, youthful energy into your heart.

Feed that desire to innovate. Everyone is born with an innate desire to create. When work, school, and life get in the way, that spark can be silenced. Make a conscious effort to fuel your creative fires. Whether writing a short story, building a treehouse, putting together a photo album, or baking an elaborate confection, when you become inspired through creating, your energy is lifted.

Listen to your inner voice. The adult, deadline-filled, "hurry-up-and-wait" world we live in creates a lot of noise that quiets your inner child. By quieting the din, you'll reconnect with your inner child and gain access into your own intuition. By removing unnecessary stressors and prioritizing what's really important, you can meet life's challenges while maintaining a child-like curiosity and lightheartedness. A playful soul is a happy soul.

According to a study by the American Academy of Pediatrics, highly scheduled children have less time for free, child-driven, creative play which offers benefits that may be protective against the effects of pressure and stress. Given this research, it just makes good sense to make playtime a priority! Is there anything more magical than placing a firefly in a jar and watching it light up as the moon smiles above? When it's spelled out like this, it's easy to see how you can raise HAPPY KIDS!

Playtime = Reduced Stress = Happy Kids. There's really no need to overcomplicate it.

H – Hoping and knowing that they will catch many fireflies

A – Anticipating nothing but success and joy in all their adventures

P – Positive that bubbles filled with wishes will fly high

P – Passionate about reaching their goals no matter how many fireflies they miss

Y – Youthful energy untainted by doubt or fear

K – Kisses and good wishes for a job well done for themselves and others

I – Imaginations growing with each leap and each wish-filled bubble

D – Deliciously surprised and satisfied by their accomplishments

S – Stress-free moments and carefree hours that add up to a lifetime of happiness

Let Little Imaginations Run Wild!

A big part of a child's healthy development involves cultivating her imagination—giving her the tools and space to immerse herself in a world that is entirely hers. It is in this space of exploration that children go through the important business of figuring out their place in the world and how they would like to maneuver in it. Imaginative play lets children reframe vital information and learn how to problem-solve.

Let your children lead the way. Ask them to plan a wellness day, or a family activity, or create a game that you can play with them. Be prepared to attend an at-home fashion show, or go on a bug hunt. Whatever it is, they will delight in their own sense of power and enjoy being the "parent" for a moment.

SANITY SAVER   A pile of colorful fabric can inspire creative play and lift your mood. Pick up rainbow colors at your local fabric store or thrift store and let the fun begin. Kids can experience playing with colors. Stand back and let their imaginations take flight as they make flags, costumes, blindfolds, and more! Have you ever tried jumping into a pile of colors?

LORI'S LESSON

I always incorporate musical instruments into my decorating, leaving them within reach of little hands. It lets children explore music in a less structured way, begin to see music as a feel-good activity, and allows them to express their inner brilliance! I have joined many an impromptu musical parade around my house. Even my teens and their friends have given in to the temptation to shake a shekere or axatse (African gourd rattles), or pick up a rainstick propelling them into a day of music making. T.J. Maxx is a great place to check for unusual, organic, and international instruments. Check in the household section; they're normally just scattered about.

Overcoming Playtime Challenges

Time and space are two obvious limiting factors when it comes to making playtime a priority in your home. Here are some ways to change your mindset if you only see obstacles on the path to playtime.

If you have limited outdoor space . . . seek out local parks, walking trails, playgrounds, and public pools.

If there are few kids in your neighborhood . . . schedule playdates. Meet halfway. Do sleepover swaps: *I keep your kids overnight, and you keep mine next time.* Join mom groups or go to Chuck E. Cheese's, or places where other children gather for impromptu socializing.

If you have a too-serious vibe in your home . . . play music from your childhood or high school days and remember what you were like before you were a parent! Tap into that free-spirited fun-loving youth. Make your home more kid friendly and fun by getting colorful inexpensive plates or putting out a playful tablecloth. Buy flowers to add a splash of color. Host a tea party where everyone wears a funny hat (dad included!).

If you have limited spending money for toys . . . have a dedicated costume box filled with thrift store finds and leftover Halloween costumes. Leave it out year-round. Bust out the towels, blankets, and sheets and use them to build forts. Save cardboard boxes for endless possibilities.

If you're overscheduled . . . block off distinct hours dedicated to playtime in your calendar. Commit to it as if it were a meeting with the CEO of your company. Relinquish commitments that no longer serve you so that you can free up time to play with your children. (Guaranteed it'll be more fulfilling!)

—— Relax FAQ ——

Q: How can I tell if my child's schedule is too stressful for him?

A: Read the cues your child is giving you. If he is whining all of the time, or otherwise indicating that he is tired; if you find yourself dragging him into the car while he's telling you he doesn't want to go; if he's having a lot of melt-downs; these are ways of telling you that he is overscheduled. Children don't have the words to convey this at their fingertips. Look at his schedule and see if you might be overdoing it for your child. Some stress is good, for example, the excitement of being in a soccer game, but stress can go too far and the inability to handle it makes a child unhappy. With this in mind, take note of your own sensibilities. If you feel you are not catching your breath or that your teeth are clenched, these are big tips that there is an imbalance that you do not want for your family life.

SANITY SAVER   When stuck in traffic with the kids or waiting on a car pool line, try playing this progressive muscle relaxation game. Ask your kids to "Tighten your jaws, your lips, and your nose. Crunch up your whole face! Squeeze them as tight as you can. Hold, hold, hold . . . and release! Ahhhhh." This may become your kid's favorite. (Muscle relaxation is explored further in *The Goodnight Caterpillar* and *Angry Octopus*.)

Above All, Have Fun!

Remove the pressure of thinking you need to constantly be providing entertainment for your child. The key is to strike a balance between giving your child unstructured playtime for him to be by himself or with siblings or friends, and enjoying playtime as a family. Following you'll find some simple, stress reducing, confidence building activities you can enjoy as a family or in a group setting.

STRESS-LESS ACTIVITY: GO FLY A KITE!

A piece of cloth connected to a string . . . in the hands of a child produces smiles, opens a world of possibilities, and decreases stress. There is something awe inspiring and exhilarating about flying a kite. Young, old, and in-between (teens) experience a sense of wonder and accomplishment when their kite takes to the air. Worries leave your mind as you focus on the magic of flight. Why not head out this weekend for a relaxation outing with your family? Go fly a kite! (Here's how to make a simple kite out of a plastic bag: *www.wikihow.com/Make-a-Kite-Out-of-a-Plastic-Bag*.)

How Kite Flying Reduces Worries:

1. **Exercise and take deep breaths.** Flying a kite can be beneficial for stress reduction. Increased blood flow and fresh air help keep bodies healthy and minds refreshed.
2. **Take your mind off your worries.** Give your brain a break and get stress relief when you focus completely on the activity at hand.
3. **Laughing induces physical changes in our body and brain.** Endorphins are released that can reduce pain and release stress. Kite entanglements create more laughter and joyful memories.
4. **Bonding with your children decreases anxiety and fear.** Spending quality-focused time with our children increases feelings of love and security.
5. **Self-esteem and confidence soar with the kite.** Children with strong self-esteem have fewer struggles with anxiety.

STRESS-LESS ACTIVITY: SATURDAY MORNING SHAKER

Start your weekend by shaking off the stress you and your children might have accumulated over the week. Make up your own tune or get inspired by *Shake Your Booty* by KC & The Sunshine Band, *Pop, Pop, Pop Those Bubbles* by Gymboree, or *The Hokey Pokey*, all found on YouTube for your listening pleasure. This is an opportunity to de-stress, connect as a family, and share. For added impact you can substitute the word *worries* with the specific stressor.

Here are examples of various ways you can sing and shake. Be sure to shake your hands, shoulders, and legs. For extra giggles shake your booty!

1. Shake, shake, shake your worries. Shake, shake, shake your worries. Shake, shake, shake your worries. Watch them go away!

2. Shake, shake, shake. Shake, shake, shake. Shake your worries. Shake your worries.
3. You throw your stress in. You throw your stress out. You throw your stress in and you shake it all about.

(This activity is taken from *Stress Free Kids® Curriculum* and works both in the classroom and in the home.)

Parent's POV
On Play as Stress Relief

"There's nothing like dancing 'round the living room to ease tension, get rid of excess energy, simply laugh, and be a bit crazy together! We love it in my house!"—Georgia

The power of play is proven. And the great thing about it is that it has the capacity to both relax your child as well as stimulate her brain. Indeed, Dr. Stuart Brown from the National Institute for Play may have said it best: "What do most Nobel Laureates, innovative entrepreneurs, artists and performers, well-adjusted children, happy couples and families, and the most successfully adapted mammals have in common? They play enthusiastically throughout their lives."

SANITY SAVER Let your kids splash in puddles, rescue worms, and dance in the rain. The very act of little feet stomping releases stress, anger, and energy. A little mud never hurt anyone and water dries!

PART II

THE ABCs OF DECREASING STRESS

*"Stress is the trash of modern life—
we all generate it but if you don't
dispose of it properly, it will
pile up and overtake your life."*

—TERRI GUILLEMETS

You'll soon see that reducing stress can be as easy as ABC for you and your family. This simple list that follows makes it fun for you and your child to pick a letter, read, and implement a tip that will reduce stress for the day.

A – Affirmations = Positive Statements = Less Stress
B – Be aware of overscheduling
C – Counteract stress with relaxation and stress-management techniques
D – Deep breathing decreases anger and anxiety
E – Exhale and say *ahhhh* . . .
F – Focus on relaxation and sleep will follow
G – Go for a slow family walk
H – Hope decreases anxiety and fear
I – Imagine a positive outcome
J – Juggle less
K – Keep it simple; keep it fun
L – Laughter is a stress reducer
M – Music calms, soothes, and uplifts
N – Negative thoughts can be replaced with positive thoughts
O – Organizing eliminates chaos and frustration
P – Playing is essential
Q – Quiet time is part of life
R – Relaxation can be incorporated into each day
S – Stop the chatter in your head
T – Teens or toddlers: We ALL need downtime
U – Understand that a stressed life means something is out of balance
V – Visualizing increases creativity
W – Waste time and be happy about it
X – XOXO kids, teens, we all relax with a hug or a kiss
Y – Young or old can learn stress management
Z – Zap stress, anxiety, fear. . . . Live in joy, hope, balance

School can open a Pandora's box of stressors for your child, and this list can be used as a powerful antidote! Fill your child's emotional backpack by sending yourself back to basics with these ABCs of decreasing stress. Together, pick a letter or start at the very beginning. Work as a parent-child team and make a commitment to reducing stress this school year. The simplicity of this list reminds both me and my children to keep it simple. By picking a letter we step into action and bring relaxation back into focus.

CHAPTER 5

Family Stress-Busters

"The quickest way for a parent to get a child's attention is to sit down and look comfortable."
—LANE OLINGHOUSE

To figure out if your family is under stress, consider these questions: Do you take a full deep breath or is your breathing shallow? Do you find yourself listening to angry self-talk? Are you always on the drive-through line for takeout? Are you happy? Are you rested? Have you confused keeping your child busy with supporting your child's happiness? Do you do anything to nourish your own soul? Do you even know who YOU are anymore? Honest answers will help you evaluate whether you're living your life in balance or if you're living out of balance. When we are out of balance we are stressed-out.

> ### Parent's POV
> #### On Balance
> "When mom feels balanced and appreciated she changes the energy of the home, her children, and how they both experience life." —Carla

In today's fast-paced, demanding society *everyone* experiences stress, so there's little hope your family can escape it altogether. But that doesn't mean the situation is hopeless! Here, you'll learn the techniques you need to help your family cope with stress in a healthy, constructive way.

I Cannot Tell a Lie . . .

There's a powerful quote by Thomas Jefferson that says, "Honesty is the first chapter of the book of wisdom." For the purposes of this book, honesty is something to be acknowledged and practiced, as it's a major steppingstone on the path to a less stressful life.

As an adult, you know how stressful it can be to be harboring a half-truth. All of the needless worry about when and how the truth may come out is enough to spike your cortisol to unhealthy levels.

Children need to learn at an early age that being truthful even in situations that may be deemed "difficult" always trumps the alternative. It may seem simple, but instilling this requires dedication on your part. However, it will pay off in spades when your children move from carefree youngsters to upstanding adults with a clean conscience throughout. Children need to know that being truthful and living an honest life feels good.

ℭ LORI'S LESSON ℈

My own daughter pierced her ears after we told her she was not allowed to. While hiding her ears for two days she became noticeably quiet and sad. She finally came clean in a sea of tears and told us what she had done. We thanked her for telling us the truth and decided to use this as a teaching moment. This valuable lesson let her feel firsthand how being untruthful negatively impacted her emotional well-being and caused her to lose sleep. She felt much better after being truthful and realized that telling the truth feels good—even if her ears were still stinging!

Imagine . . .
Close your eyes, take a deep breath, and imagine what it would feel like to live an honest life.

Here are a few key ingredients to keep your home full of honest vibrations and to build lasting, happy memories with your family (unsullied by stress):

- Good communication that's safe, loving, and honest.
- Mutual respect and trust.
- Clear and reasonable expectations.
- An attitude of teamwork.

You're Only Human!

At some point on your parenting journey, you're bound to feel a sense of fatigue or even sleep deprivation. *(I assure you this is entirely normal—you're in good company.)* The key is to identify these feelings before they spiral into emotions that can have negative consequences for you and your family. A lack of sleep can wear down even the most Zen-minded parent causing irritability, memory loss, and lack of coordination. Sleep deprivation can lead to such health problems as heart disease, diabetes, obesity, and depression. Let's face it: There is a fine line between fatigue and deprivation and your parenting sanity and emotional stability depend on it! When your mind and body are screaming for rest, you must rest. In the pages of this book, you'll discover how breathing, affirmations, visualizations, and progressive muscle relaxation can be used to transform your sleep.

Here are some signs that you're suffering from parenting fatigue, as broken down by family coach and author, Ronae Jull:

- You can't recall the last time you truly enjoyed spending time with your kids.
- You can't recall the last time you did something just for *you* without feeling guilty.
- You struggle to just make it through your days, grateful for any conflict-free moment.
- You resent having to balance all the different "hats" you wear.
- You struggle with anger, depression, or anxiety.
- You constantly feel mentally, physically, or spiritually drained.

If more than half of this list resonates with you, you're definitely fatigued.

The Antidote? A Shift in Focus

When you take each day as it comes, being mindful of ways to refill your heart, you will rediscover the joy in parenting even if you have a challenging child or you're going through a challenging time at home. Who you are is more than your parenting role, although that role is a big part of your life. Find support, ask for help when you feel overwhelmed, and be vigilant about carving out time for the things that take care of YOU. (*Indigo Dreams: Adult Relaxation* is designed for you. The techniques will help you achieve a deep state of sleep so that you can feel refreshed in the morning.)

Remember when your child was first born, and those overwhelming first days and weeks? You made it through. This time is no different. You'll make it through! And your child will grow up to be an adult who has to make her own mistakes and learn from them. By being intentional about refilling your heart, you will be able to enjoy the journey. When you keep the essence of YOU intact, you give your child the gift of your uniqueness. Children want to see the real you, the magnificent you, not just the exhausted parenting you. When you love yourself, your children learn self-love.

MINDFUL MANTRA

Just for today, I will be gentle with myself.
I love myself enough to rest.

LORI'S LESSON

When I am in my car stopped at a red light, I entertain the kids (and especially my teens) by looking at myself in the mirror and giving myself compliments. I say, "I love my hair, I love my arms, I love my fingers, I love my wrinkles." Who cares if they mock me? I know they are getting the message on a deeper level. Mission accomplished!

Walking the (Positive) Talk

You likely have a running mental dialogue going on in your head that tells you what you could have, should have, or would have done better. Simultaneously you hear a list of what you need to do in the next minute or hour, or perhaps criticism for what you're doing wrong in this very moment. Walking the talk not only quiets the chatter of negative self-talk that keeps you exhausted, but it helps makes life feel lighter and more enjoyable. You'll soon see that adopting such habits as affirmations is more akin to running a marathon, not a sprint. By putting in the "training," your family will be rewarded with better health and a more relaxed lifestyle—something that definitely justifies the effort!

As a family, use affirmations or positive statements regularly to counteract stress and promote healing and optimism. Teach your children to take a break and say, "I am calm. I am healthy. I am peaceful. I am happy. I am strong." Write positive statements with your children so they can carry one in their pocket for the day. Use an arts and crafts moment for your kids to make signs for their rooms. Put happy healing notes for them to discover under their pillows or in their lunchboxes. (*Affirmation Weaver,* found on *Indigo Ocean Dreams* CD is a story that introduces children to positive statements.)

STRESS-LESS ACTIVITY: CREATE AN AFFIRMATION BOWL

To help your children get in the habit of thinking positively, here's a fun activity to do together.

Materials:
- Fish bowl (or colorful plastic pasta bowl)
- Colored paper
- Markers, crayons, or colored pencils
- Scissors

Activity:

1. As a family, sit down and brainstorm a long list of positive affirmations, or type up a bunch on a list for kids to cut out, such as: "I am full of good ideas," "I am very creative," "I am unique and valuable," etc.

2. Write several affirmations on the sheets of colored paper.

3. Cut them out, fold them up, and put them in the bowl. Display the bowl in a place that's easy for everyone in your family to access.

4. Before anyone leaves the house for the day, or together as a family at breakfast, make sure everyone picks one affirmation to read aloud and focus on as a way to set a positive tone for the day.

Here are a few affirmations to get you started:

- I see the good in me.
- I am ready to learn.
- I love my teacher.
- I am fun.
- I like myself.
- I make friends easily.
- I am happy.
- I believe in myself.

Parent's POV
On Remaining Optimistic

"I think that fostering optimism in children is one of the greatest tools you can give [kids] to succeed in life. One of the things that I do with my son at night as we are going to bed is talk about the events of the day and what we're happiest about. It is a lot of fun and really keeps him focused on the good things that happened throughout the day." —Erin

Ꮧ LORI'S LESSON Ꮧ

As a young, overwhelmed, sleep-deprived mom, I realized I was exposing my children to my struggles via less-than-positive statements. When my 5-year-old daughter dropped her crayon during breakfast, I heard her say from under the table, "I am having a miserable day already." I knew she was repeating something she heard me say and it broke my heart. I made the commitment to become more aware of adopting an optimistic attitude and adding positive words to my world.

A Breath of Fresh Air

Breathing is a natural antidote to stress, anxiety, anger, and exhaustion. Breath awareness is a magnificent internal gift that you can always rely on to feel better. Practice controlled breathing with your family. Taking slow deep breaths can help reduce your child's anxiety and anger. It is also recommended for pain management as well as a way for you to self-regulate. If you focus on your breathing you will be better able to respond to, instead of reacting to, any situation. Please know that a relaxed parent makes better decisions, relaxed teens makes better choices, and a relaxed child is a blessing. For added impact, have your children visualize breathing in joy-filled air!

Note: Don't wait for a meltdown to teach deep breathing. That's like trying to close the hurricane windows during the hurricane. Just as you would prepare for a hurricane on a sunny, beautiful, still day, you can prepare for stress, anger, and anxiety with your child on a poised, peaceful day. Explore relaxation techniques before the storm.

All family members can benefit from this important and powerful stress-management technique. It's also extremely effective for diffusing anger. Children can use breathing when they start to feel overstimulated or on the verge of a temper tantrum; merely have them focus on their breathing and soothe themselves.

Breathe in, 2, 3, 4, and out, 2, 3, 4. In, 2, 3, 4, and out, 2, 3, 4.
For added impact say *"Ahhhh"* **. . . as you exhale.**

Encourage your child to show one of her dolls or stuffed animals this technique. (Kids love to breathe with the sea otters in *Sea Otter Cove*.) During stress-free moments, ask your child how focusing on breathing changes the way that she feels. Ask her how she thinks she can apply this to her life.

STRESS-LESS ACTIVITY: BREATHING LESSONS

Chill a mirror in the refrigerator for at least an hour. Take it out and let your kids fog it up by exhaling their breath onto the cold mirror. Let them use their fingers to write the word "relax," draw a smile, or even a full "I am calm" sentence onto the mirror. The power of breathing becomes tangible.

SANITY SAVER   Use deep breathing with your children to decrease test-taking anxiety, self-regulate, soothe hyperactivity, or release anger. Breathing deeply can promote clear thinking during frustrating homework moments, and nurture sweet dreams.

Don't Forget Dad

Today's dads should not be overlooked in this family equation. This quote by Dr. David Popenoe sums it up so well: "Fathers are far more than just 'second adults' in the home. Involved fathers bring positive benefits to their children that no other person is as likely to bring."

Dads are an impressive group who, for the most part, are the first generation of men to change diapers, take their daughters to dance class, and cook dinner—most without having witnessed their own fathers being so involved! They are technology savvy and actively use Facebook and Twitter to reach out and support each » other. Like many moms, today's dads are stressed-out. Remember: A calm dad also contributes to a peaceful family. Here are some ways dads (especially stay-at-home dads) can recharge their batteries, as suggested by Michael Lawrience in a guest post on my site, found here: *www.stressfreekids.com/10234/stress-relievers-for-men*:

- Exercising
- Hanging out with their guy friends
- Finding alone time
- Building relationships (online or in person) with other dads
- Engaging in stress-relief techniques (e.g., deep breathing or yoga)
- Going on a date with their wife (without the kids)
- Reading
- Incorporating positive character-building statements (e.g., "I am emotionally available to my family and friends.")

Dads, take a cue from your kids and play one of their video games with them for a few minutes. Scientists at East Carolina University looked at how adults' levels of tension, depression, and anger were affected by gaming and saw vast improvements among the study participants. While we do not want to encourage more screen time, playing in your child's world can be very valuable.

⚜ LORI'S LESSON ⚜

Building a relationship with our children is our responsibility. I applaud my husband for creating his own special bonding moments with our children. When I get out of the way, it gives my husband freedom to develop his own unique relationship with our kids. I had a small victory when my daughter told me that her dad could not join me to walk the dog because they were "bonding." Don't you just love it when your kids "get it"?

**STRESS-LESS ACTIVITY:
RELATIONSHIP BUILDER DAD WILL LOVE!**

The Home Depot stores offer free, how-to workshops designed for ages 5–12. Dads can take advantage of this once-a-month opportunity to connect with his child. Accompanied by an adult your child gets to build objects that can be used around the home or community. Each child receives a resounding dose of self-confidence and a kid-sized orange apron.

Parent's POV
On "Dad" Time and Staying Sane

"As the dad of six kids, three daughters-in-law, a soon-to-be daughter-in-law, and two dogs . . . I can attest to taking time out to go to the gym. It makes it possible to give more at home and is a critical mental health component to my life. A side note is that it's a great place to build friendships as well." —Rusty

Painting a (Positive) Picture with Your Mind

It is both fun and effective to create a visualization or use your imagination to paint a positive picture with your mind. Create a go-to happy thought that children can think of when they are stressed or worried. Develop a short story or scene that your child can access when he is fearful or anxious. Children can implement this new self-soothing skill during doctor or dentist visits. Even going for a haircut can be more enjoyable when your child employs their happy thought visualization. Go for a tranquil ride on a cloud or float in a bubble. Slide down a rainbow and encourage children to create their own relaxation story. Write the story down or record it. Now the kids can help mom and dad get relaxed with their very own story. (*Bubble Riding* is a story that shows children how to visualize.)

— Relax FAQ —

Q: My daughter's big fear is new things and future events; after all, anxiety is worry about the future. What would you recommend for her issues?

A: Try creating a visualization or story for her in which she steps into the unknown and it's a safe, friendly, warm, and welcoming place. You can create the framework and then she can add to it or come up with her very own story. You can also create affirmations to reinforce this. For example, she could say, "Tomorrow will bring new and wonderful surprises. The unknown is a safe, loving space filled with adventure."

STRESS-LESS ACTIVITY: STOP THE CHATTER

1. Focus on an image such as a flower or a candle. Set a timer for thirty seconds or even less and try to think only of that image. When you become comfortable with thirty seconds increase your time until you achieve one minute. Let your children try this with you. Kids will see it as a game (the "focus game") and time spent with mom or dad.

2. Focus on a color with your eyes open. It can be a sheet of construction paper, a screen saver, or crayon. If a thought enters your head, simply acknowledge the thought and send it away. Increase participation by letting your child set the timer.

3. Close your eyes and focus on a color. Once you get to this level you will be able to apply this technique anytime. This is an extremely helpful relaxation technique to stop the chatter and help you and your children fall asleep. *(I often fall asleep by filling my brain with a color. Sometimes it is the only way I can stop the chatter.)*

4. Focusing on a color or image is a form of visualizing. (*Indigo Dreams CD Series* introduces this very technique to all ages. *A Boy and a Turtle* and *Bubble Riding* are two stories that use color for visualizing.)

Raising Optimistic Children

Much stress, anxiety, fear, and even depression occur because we are conditioned to expect a negative outcome. Many of you are able to jump to the worst negative outcome in a single bound. Children are hopeful by nature but are quickly influenced by adult ways. Paying attention to your thoughts and expectations and tweaking them with optimism can produce dramatic results. Leading by example and seeing the positive side of life experiences aids in cementing this concept in your child's mind.

ꙮ LORI'S LESSON ꙮ

"WHAT IF the pole falls on your car when we go into the store, Miss Lori?" 9-year-old Jane asked me as I parked the car in front of a large utility pole. "Hmmm . . . What if it doesn't and we come out to find the car exactly the way we left it?" I responded. We both smiled, let out a sigh of relief, and off we went.

Parent's POV
On Ingraining the Positive

"I've got two kids in therapy. Truly this one little 'What If?' trick has had more of an impact than all the therapy they've had so far. The difference in my daughter's anxiety since we started practicing it has been huge. On the way to school she told me she'd seen a commercial for a scary movie before bed last night and it freaked her out, but she decided to shift her focus to: 'What if that is just a movie, and not real?' Doing this allowed her to calm herself and go to sleep. This is a game-changer in our house—a way to focus on positive possibilities instead of fear about negative ones that usually never happen!" —Michelle

What If?

Two of the most powerful words happen to be **WHAT IF?** . . . When you ask the world, or yourself **"WHAT IF?"**, you have the power to answer your own question with a positive outcome—or a negative outcome. Unfortunately, many of you likely find it easier to fill in the blanks with negative, anxiety-causing outcomes. And children are even more creative, with many eager to fill in the blanks with kid-style anxiety-causing outcomes that will never materialize.

"What if we fall in the lake and get bit by a fish?"

"What if a monster is lurking under the bed?"

"What if no one likes me?"

This negative self-talk creates anxiety and keeps happiness at bay. When you couple **WHAT IF?** with positive, hopeful outcomes you can reduce anxiety and experience calm and joy. **WHAT IF?** is a simple phrase that becomes an effective stress-management, optimism building technique for the entire family.

"What if I sit by the lake and have fun?"

"What if monsters are only pretend?"

"What if everyone likes me and I make new friends?"

Observe and listen to your family. You will be amazed at all the **WHAT IF?** scenarios you and your children can come up with in a twenty-four-hour period.

Take the **WHAT IF?** challenge! The next time you hear your kids or yourself filling in the blanks with negative words . . . take a moment . . . take a breath . . . smile . . . and finish your question with an affirmative outcome.

MINDFUL MANTRA

Just for today, I will be hopeful. I expect positive outcomes and inspire my family to focus on the positive with me.

CHAPTER 6

Tools to Tackle Stress

"It's not the load that breaks you down, it's the way you carry it."

—LENA HORNE

✑ LORI'S LESSON ✑

My shoulders ached, I lost weight, I couldn't sleep, and I found myself holding my breath. I was constantly expecting the worst-case scenario and felt bitter, resentful, and unhappy. The day I doubled over in the school parking lot from yet another stress attack, I knew I had to make a change. I added breathing, positive statements, visualizing, and muscle relaxation to my life. Then I picked up a canvas and paintbrush . . .

Among the myriad ways to beat back the harmful effects of stress, here you'll find those that work time and time again. They deserve special placement in your arsenal of stress-busting techniques because they are so effective! Use them liberally throughout your days and they'll become an integral part of your family's new stress-free story.

Tool #1: Creating Art

Exploring art presents the perfect way to connect with your children. Turn screens off and color or paint. Encourage your kids to notice how they feel when they paint or draw with different colors. Some colors feel relaxing, some promote joy, while others express anger. Let children relieve stress by doodling or coloring a mandala . . . no rules . . . just relaxing and expressing. Sand art or sand painting brings additional new elements into your field of exploration. The Drepung Loseling monks travel the world sharing their sand mandala creation process. They believe that when children see their sand mandala they receive a positive imprint that germinates as sprouts of peace as they grow older. Navajo Indians used sand painting as part of their elaborate healing ceremonies. Add music and let children sample how listening to various types of music while creating affects their art. Take your art-making outside. Make sculptures out of rocks or pinecones, make a labyrinth out of acorns or gravel—art projects don't require expensive supplies. Part of the fun is getting creative with what you have lying around the house or in your yard! It can be as simple as filling a bucket with water and painting the sidewalk with water. If your child has pent-up energy or anger, fill a sock with broken pieces of chalk. Tie a knot on the end and let your child bang it against the sidewalk or toss the sock up into the air. Let your child make suggestions. Art feeds self-esteem.

Parent's POV
On Imaginative Play

"With twenty years of working with children, nearly everything I have taught involves imaginative play. My play kit consists of empty boxes, puppets, clothes for dress up, books, and arts and crafts. Open-ended play in which they move from one thing to the next in their own imaginative world is simply amazing. I love being caught up in their enthusiasm and I learn so much from them too." —Natalie

Tool #2: Listening to Music

Music reduces stress and can be used to relax, inspire, motivate, focus, and heal. You educate your children by incorporating music into their lives as this is a powerful emotional management tool.

Music is considered to be therapeutic and its benefits are being explored with cancer patients, the elderly with Alzheimer's, and children with Autism Spectrum Disorder. Casually exposing your children to music shows them how vibrations and sound can change the way they feel, function, and respond to stressful situations. Music can even help them focus on their homework. Adding music can help to lift your spirit and become your children's go-to tool throughout their lives. Relaxation music is particularly soothing and can positively affect their brain, lower their blood pressure, alleviate pain, reduce stress, and boost their immune systems. (*Indigo Dreams: Rainforest Relaxation Music* combines music with the sounds of nature.)

Because music changes your physiology (for the better), you can also look at music through the lens of science. Ask your children to notice how they feel when they listen to or play music. Ask them:

- Is your heart rate slowing down?
- Has your breathing changed?
- Do you feel like you can think more clearly?
- Do you feel happy or sleepy from this music?
- Does this type of music distract you or help you concentrate?

Parent's POV
On Music and Focus

"I have found that 'chill' music played just loud enough so that students have to strain to hear it helps greatly. Students straining to hear the music somehow tend to focus on the learning and produce good work." —Robert

Perhaps try playing with the science of sound. Talk about the rainforest . . . play rainforest relaxation music . . . study ocean sounds . . . play sounds of whales and dolphins, and see how your children respond. Study weather patterns . . . explore the sounds of gentle wind and rain. See what this stirs up in your kids, while watching them take in the soothing energy of the natural rhythms. (*Indigo Dreams: Kid's Relaxation Music* inspires and relaxes.)

Imagine . . .

Close your eyes, take a deep breath, and imagine the music notes washing through you and over you. Feel yourself melt as you sink into a soothing rhythm that creates harmony in your mind and body.

Tool #3: Writing

Creative writing offers unlimited opportunities to write various stories with themes of relaxation, motivation, or amazing positive outcomes. (This is particularly useful if your child is experiencing a recurring nightmare. Have him write his nightmare and create a pleasant and reassuring ending.) Journaling can increase self-care awareness. Children can note one thing that made them feel content, or hopeful, or grateful. Gratitude is an uplifting stress-buster. Starting your day by writing down something you are grateful for can change the entire mood of the day.

You can also use writing to let go of resentments, hurt feelings, or anger. Have your child write something she wants to get rid of on a piece of paper. Have her crumble it up, tear it to pieces, or stamp on it. For extra oomph, roll it into a ball and toss it across the room into a trash can. If she misses the can enough, she'll probably start laughing, which will add yet another stress-buster to the exercise. Kids that can laugh at themselves have more resilience.

MINDFUL MANTRA

Just for today, I will rewrite my parenting story. I find freedom in knowing that each day is a new beginning.

SANITY SAVER   Create a "Stop the Mind List." Instead of remembering everything you need to do, write it down or keep a list in your phone and give yourself permission to stop playing the list over and over again in your mind. When the list starts up, acknowledge the thought and send the thought away. Reducing the constant reminders in your head will free up brain space for serenity.

Tool #4: Dancing

Whether you enroll in a dance class as a family, or you enjoy impromptu dance parties regularly in your living room, moving your body develops coordination, offers emotional release, helps blow off steam, and reduces stress! Little ones can particularly benefit from this as they often have energy to spare, so channeling it in this fun freeform way encourages them to get moving, and explore sounds and the space around them.

Music and dance are a universal language. Sneak in some stress- and anger-reducing moves by shaking your stress out and stomping your anger away. Or, pretend you are in a bubble and you cannot let your bubbles bump into each other. Use dancing as an opportunity to integrate a teaching moment—spatial awareness is an important social skill.

STRESS-LESS ACTIVITY: HOST A FAMILY TALENT SHOW

Every so often plan an evening where each member of the family can show off his or her musical or dancing abilities! This can be as elaborate or as simple as you want it to be. If you're in the mood to really play it up, you can have your kids create flyers and invite friends. But it really can be as simple as lip-synching to a favorite tune, demonstrating some Tai Chi forms, or even doing a magic trick and inviting everyone to clap along! (*The Perfect Club* found on *Indigo Dreams: Garden of Wellness* CD will inspire your talent show and give the kids some ideas.)

⤳ LORI'S LESSON ⤲

I was at an amusement park with a group of children. One of the children was challenged by the sounds, activities, excitement, and visual chaos. I asked him if he would like to take a brain break, and he said yes. I suggested that he focus his gaze on the yellow piece of popcorn on the ground and take some deep breaths. After a minute I asked him if he was feeling calmer and he said yes. I let him know that he can take this sort of brain break whenever he felt like he wanted to be the boss of his brain and energy.

Tool #5: Taking Brain Breaks

When that overwhelmed feeling strikes, it's incredibly soothing and healthful to take a "brain break," which basically entails stopping whatever activity you are currently engaged in and giving yourself a breather. With kids (especially younger children), you may need to look for signs that they are in need of a brain break and announce to them that downtime is needed for a few minutes.

Here are twelve easy things you can suggest your child do when she needs to decompress:

1. Buzz like a bee.
2. Hum.
3. Focus on breathing.
4. Turn off all screens.
5. Drive with the radio off to enjoy silence.
6. Press mute during TV commercials.
7. Doodle aimlessly.
8. Run fingers through a bowl of uncooked rice.
9. Roll a tennis ball underfoot.
10. Explore pressure points: Adjust the pose on *The Thinker* statue; instead rest forehead on your hand.
11. Implement face yoga. Lion Face or Horse Lips are two poses to get you started.
12. Hold a smooth rock in your hand or squeeze a stress ball.

Whether you need the brain break or your child needs a brain break, announce that you are taking a brain break. It will become a familiar phrase that can trigger a relaxation response.

—— **Relax FAQ** ——

Q: My child gets antsy sitting at the table doing homework after school, and I'm not sure how to help her settle down and focus on her studies. What do you recommend?

A: Allow your daughter to change things up by doing her homework outside or moving from area to area. After all, it doesn't matter one bit where it gets done so long as it gets done with the least amount of stress incurred. The sunshine, fresh air, and change of scenery may be enough to help her zone in on the topic at hand. You're also giving her a sense of autonomy by letting her explore and see firsthand what works and doesn't work. Try dropping the traditional ideas of homework being tied to a desk or table. It'll likely result in a much happier experience for all involved.

Tool #6: Gardening and Getting Out in Nature

The National Gardening Association says that the act of gardening benefits kids' health, well-being, and attitude towards learning. This stress-reducing activity also builds self-esteem and creativity while fostering bonds with nature and family. If you don't have space for a garden, you can join a community or co-op garden. You'll reap all the benefits of gardening and make new friends too. What's not to love?

ℰ𝒻 LORI'S LESSON ℛℴ

I watched my daughter plan, select, and plant a small flower garden with her friend. A few days later she and her dad planted tomato and cucumber seeds at my kitchen table. Dirt was spilt as planning and laughing ensued. My husband and daughter side by side; two mad scientists bonding, scheming, and planting not just cucumber seeds . . . but seeds of joy and memories. By being a silent observer, I gave them the freedom and space to create their own tradition. Each year, I know that it is growing season when they dump dirt on my table. I have learned to love the dirt and all it represents, knowing that both the seeds and their relationship are growing deep roots of stability.

There are so many healthful benefits to gardening that it's hard to narrow down the list, but here are eleven ways having your kids grow vegetables and flowers contributes to their overall well-being. Gardening:

1. Gives kids a sense of pride and accomplishment.
2. Creates bonding opportunities with parents, siblings, and friends.
3. Reduces stress.
4. Gives kids outdoor physical activity.
5. Encourages healthy eating.
6. Increases responsibility.
7. Creates environmental awareness.
8. Teaches nurturing and patience.
9. Stimulates a desire to learn.
10. Increases self-esteem and creativity.
11. Plants a relaxation seed that will grow when you least expect it.

No Green Thumb? No Problem!

Even if you've never grown vegetables or you only have space for growing in containers or a very small garden plot, try this rewarding outdoor activity with your children. It can be a learning experience for you all. Here are some very simple guidelines for keeping it all stress free:

- Remember: Vegetables and flowers are resilient and gardening does not need to be perfect. Let your kids make mistakes. Whatever you plant will grow anyway!
- Keep your kids motivated by planting quick-growing veggies such as corn, cucumbers, sunflowers, and radishes.
- Foster independence and creativity. Allow your kids to choose what to grow and let them help design your garden plot or pick colorful pots for planting.

- Grow herbs. Choose a few your kids can pick such as basil and oregano, which you can add to sauces, dips, and stews. Grow lavender for its relaxation properties. Kids can pick and place fresh lavender near their pillows.
- Cultivate responsibility. Help your kids create a schedule for watering and weed control.
- Try indoor plants, too—especially if you have limited or no outdoor space. Venus flytraps, terrariums, or Chia Pets provide similar benefits. Even growing a bean in a jar is magical for little ones!

SANITY SAVER   No gardening space? No worries. Urbio offers indoor gardening containers that turn your wall into a garden, making green spaces available to anyone. Visit *www.myurbio.com*.

Did You Know?

- Children with ADHD benefit from access to green spaces. The greener the space the better the children's functioning.
- Garden therapy has been adapted to almost every kind of medical situation and social service.
- Children with access to green outdoor spaces play more creatively and score higher on tests of self-discipline.
- A study done by Kaiser Permanente showed the brain wave activity of a gardener mirrored that of someone praying or meditating.
- Neighborhoods that have gardens may see a decrease in crime. Buildings with little or no vegetation compared to buildings with high levels of greenery had 48 percent fewer property crimes and 56 percent fewer violent crimes.

MINDFUL MANTRA

*Just for today, I will connect with nature
and nurture my own growth.*

Tool #7: Cooking Together

Cooking with your children is an amazing way to create deep bonds and memories especially when you are cooking with veggies that you grew together in the garden. Many cultures consider food to be a representation of love and security. Families and even entire villages congregate around meals. Elders and today's chefs talk about the importance of infusing their food with love. You may already think of your kitchen as the heart of your home. When you introduce your children to the joys of turning wholesome ingredients into satisfying meals, you are not only setting them up for a lifetime of healthy habits, you are able to connect with your children in a way that's intimate—and ultimately delicious! Confirm your commitment to cooking with your children by stocking your kitchen with aprons for each family member.

LORI'S LESSON

When I cook, I wear my grandmother's apron. My husband wears his chef jacket and our youngest family member would wear a handmade apron created by fastening a potholder to a dishtowel. Family traditions like our secret lasagna recipe and our handmade apron have been passed down from child to child. Stress-free directions to make this heirloom apron can be found at www.flexibledreams.com/2011/01/i-heart-this-apron.html.

MINDFUL MANTRA

Just for today, I will cook with love and be mindful of enjoying this cooking experience with my children.

Remember that positive statements can be woven into any situation. Even cooking in the kitchen.

Here are some to get you going:

I nourish my body by making healthy food choices.
Cooking and eating healthy foods help me feel good.
Healthy food helps me grow big and strong.

SANITY SAVER   Relaxation Recipe:
Take 3 deep breaths
Add 1 large happy thought
Let steep for 2 minutes
Enjoy!

Tool #8: Laughing Together

Did you know that laughter can actually extend your life? Studies show that it can add eight years to your life! The sound of giggling children should be reason enough to encourage a lighthearted vibe in your home, but here are several more reasons to add laughter to your family's stress tool kit.

LAUGH FOR LESS STRESS—AND BETTER HEALTH!
When You Laugh, You . . .

- Release endorphins, which are your body's feel-good chemicals.
- Benefit from improved circulation.
- Increase immune cells and decrease stress hormones—both of which help you resist disease.

- Give your internal organs a massage.
- Have a hard time staying angry, anxious or sad; a good chuckle helps you move through an emotional state.
- Relax *and* recharge, allowing you to both calm down and get energized (the perfect combination for focus).
- Get out of your head and into your body. Laughing also encourages you to be more spontaneous.
- May release deeply held emotions, which often rise to the surface during a good belly laugh. This is not only cathartic, but makes you feel loads lighter!

Milton Berle may have said it best: "Laughter is an instant vacation." So before you waste another day, watch a funny video on YouTube or even sign up for a laughter yoga class. Encourage your family to enjoy it all along with you and see who has the last laugh!

Tool #9: Unplugging and Opening a Book

Reading for relaxation is an often overlooked, but extremely valuable, stress-management tool for children. A good story of triumph can brighten the eyes of any child. Reading gives your children a chance to stop their mind list and quiet the chatter in their brains. They can retreat to a quiet spot to relax and read, or enjoy the quiet energy of a library away from the everyday static of screens. The very act of reading a book to your children creates lifelong bonds and moments of mindful relaxation. Reading a relaxing book (such as *A Boy and a Turtle*) adds a double dose of tranquility.

STRESS-LESS ACTIVITY: CREATE A RELAXATION OASIS

Help your child enjoy downtime when she feels too revved up, tired, stressed, or angry. Your child can learn to recognize when she can benefit from going to her relaxation space—a special retreat area that you create together! The space can be defined with a simple bean bag chair or colored rug square. You can bond with your child as she decides what kinds of things she'd like to include in her relaxation oasis. Perhaps her favorite relax-activity is doing a puzzle, or listening to music and reading. Stock the space only with the items that truly facilitate relaxation for your little one. Fill the area with soothing visuals—consider including such items as a small fish tank, a snow globe, a large hourglass, or even an ant farm.

Here's how you can create your own Relaxation Bottle.

Materials:
- Empty water or pop bottles of various sizes
- Water
- Food coloring
- Glitter

1. Fill the empty bottle with food coloring, glitter, and water.
2. Swirl it and watch the glitter fall slowly. So peaceful!

Tool #10: Getting Enough Sleep

You know how stressed-out and tired you feel on the days following a night of little sleep? Well, a child that does not get adequate rest may not simply be tired—but overtired. He may react the opposite of an adult and may even become hyperactive. You will notice your child is quicker to anger, cries more easily, and may even act out aggressively. Children naturally need more sleep than adults. *(In Chapter 9, I'll get more into specific techniques for making bedtime a peaceful time in your home.)*

If your child has trouble falling asleep, you can use a proven technique called progressive muscle relaxation to help him drift off each night. You can help your child quiet his mind and body by having him actively tense and then relax various muscle groups. For a passive approach, tensing of muscles is not required. You simply send the suggestion or command of relaxation to each body part. For example this excerpt from *The Goodnight Caterpillar* shows you the exact dialogue needed. "I am going to relax my legs. I will relax my legs. My legs are relaxing. My legs are relaxed." For a variation, try an active version of the progressive muscular relaxation technique. Tighten muscle groups and relax. "Hold, hold, hold . . . *Ahhhhh . . .*"

Start with your child's feet and work your way up to his head (or reverse the order). After a few times of doing this, your little one will be one step closer to being able to use this technique on his own.

All about Sleep

Q: **What is the biggest thing that prevents kids from getting a great quality night's sleep?**

A: Brain chatter, worry, and excitement prevent children from falling asleep. Most adults do not know how to stop the chatter in their brains at bedtime. Children have the same challenge.

Q: **What are most families doing wrong when it comes to sleep for their kids?**

A: Many parents themselves have anxiety about getting their children to sleep, leaving them alone, how dark the room should be, rocking their child to sleep, and more. Children pick up on their parents' emotions and quickly deduce that there must be something scary or stressful about going to sleep. Sleeping is a natural act—the more anxious we get about it the more children sense that this is a difficult process.

Q: **Does diet or exercise have anything to do with sleep?**

A: Diet can absolutely affect sleep. Chemicals, dyes, additives, and sugar are all ingredients that can stress the body out ❯❯

and interfere with sleep. When children are stressed it means something is out of balance. Food can throw children out of balance very easily. Children need nutritious foods for their minds and bodies to run properly. Parents may want to consider vitamins or minerals geared towards relaxing the nervous system if their child is having difficulty sleeping. Calcium, magnesium, EFAs, and Vitamin B are all useful in helping to regulate your emotions and soothe nerves. Exercise is great for so many reasons, but not right before bed. Kids benefit from having a winding down period before they get ready for bed.

Q: **What can you do if your child wakes in the middle of the night?**

A: Children that wake during the night are often stressed during the day. Getting stress under control is paramount. Children can even develop stress-related night terrors. Balancing life and spending quality time helps children to sleep more soundly. Eating healthy and establishing a peaceful loving bedtime help to eliminate waking up in the middle of the night. Children can also rely on themselves to turn on relaxation music or practice their relaxation techniques in order to fall back to sleep.

Q: **What can parents change TONIGHT to help their kids sleep better?**

A: Parents can change the way they look at bedtime. Are they trying to get their kids to sleep quickly or are they bonding and helping their child relax? Teaching children to focus on their breathing or stop the chatter in their heads with visualizations can help immediately. Focus on relaxation and sleep will follow.

> *Imagine . . .*
> Close your eyes, take a deep breath, and imagine bringing down the energy of your entire home at bedtime . . . lower lights . . . slower movements . . . lower voice. . . . Have your children imagine they are powering down for the evening.

The following excerpt comes from the book, *Sea Otter Cove: A Relaxation Story,* and is also found on the *Indigo Ocean Dreams* CD. It's an effective way of shifting your child into slower, gentler bedtime energy.

The sea child told the sea otter to breathe in through his nose and out through his nose. He focused all of his attention on the tip of his nose.
They both did this breathing together.
Breathe in through your nose and out through your nose.
In, 2, 3, 4 . . . out, 2, 3, 4. In, 2, 3, 4 . . . out, 2, 3, 4.

The sea child told the sea otter that he could breathe this way whenever he felt angry or scared or nervous. He could focus on the air moving in and out of the tip of his nose, and he could feel calm. The sea otter placed his hands on his belly, and felt it lift up and down as the air moved in and out. For a few moments they both did this breathing together.
Breathe in through your nose and out through your nose.
In, 2, 3, 4 . . . out, 2, 3, 4. In, 2, 3, 4 . . . out, 2, 3, 4.

What about Meditation?

Meditation is a difficult concept to teach children. A child cannot—and should not—be forced to learn to meditate. It can take a lifetime for meditators to be able to clear their minds of all thoughts with the purpose of transcending the mind and it is impractical to impose these expectations on a child. The pursuit to learn to meditate is a very personal decision coupled with a strong commitment and desire to do so. Instead, you can focus on introducing techniques to children so that they can integrate practical tools like visualizing, breathing, and positive statements into their lives. These types of little exposures can begin at any age! Show your children how you use relaxation throughout your day. Take deep breaths when you are driving or rushing to get out the door. Try a candlelight dinner or breakfast. See who can hold their gaze on the flame for thirty seconds. Explain to your children that you are calming yourself down or use positive statements when you are feeling frustrated. With a little practice, relaxation techniques will become second nature to you and your children and if your children ever decide to give meditation a try, it will be that much easier for them to obtain a blissful meditative state.

Parent's POV
On Kids Adopting Meditation

"We teach relaxation for childbirth, and it occurred to me this summer that we should *really* be teaching these strategies to our children. It was a pleasant surprise to see our oldest child teaching her 5-year-old old and 3-year-old brothers how to chant 'OM' the other morning. It warmed my heart and reinforced what I suspected: Our children can benefit from learning relaxation strategies!" —Kristina

CHAPTER 7

Constructively Handling Anger

> *"Do not teach your children never to be angry;*
> *teach them how to be angry."*
>
> —LYMAN ABBOTT

℃ LORI'S LESSON ℃

My friend's 5-year-old son became angry and he told me that he was going to destroy my house. He started to throw some of my things around. I firmly told him that he was not allowed to hurt anyone or anything in my house, but he could yell and scream and stomp his feet for two minutes. I set the oven timer and told him to be as angry as he wanted until the bell rings. He wore himself out in a minute and wanted to shut the timer off. I let him do so; we took some deep breaths together and I let him know that I was glad he was feeling better. I explained that anytime he felt angry at my house he could set the timer, stomp it out, or take deep breaths.

Kids get mad and that's okay. But most kids don't have the experience or self-control to know how to deal with their anger. As parents, it's up to you to teach them to diffuse their anger and help them channel it in a productive way—and it all starts with your actions. Your actions demonstrate how to deal with frustrations. If kids see you responding to a potentially volatile situation with a serene and measured attitude, they will adopt a similar behavior. Above all, the important message you need to convey to your children is this:

It's okay to be angry. Anger is a normal part of life. What's absolutely NOT okay is to harm yourself, someone else, or destroy property.

SANITY SAVER   Keep things in perspective. Not every challenge or situation is an emergency.

While teaching children ways of reducing anger in a healthy manner can be challenging, children who don't learn to manage anger can suffer from emotional, physical, and social consequences. Therefore, it's your duty as a parent to give your children anger-management skills so they can cope with the frustrations of life.

STRESS-LESS ACTIVITY:
THE "LET IT GO" BUBBLE EXERCISE

Letting go of anger is challenging for children, teens, and adults. I created a visualization that involves placing the "letting-go situation" into a bubble and sending it away. This visualization, for all ages, is a wonderful way to get rid of negative feelings. The following *Bubble Blowing* exercise is an excerpt taken from *Indigo Dreams: Garden of Wellness* CD.

Imagine that you have a bubble wand in your hand. Blow a bubble. See your bubble in your mind. Can you see your bubble? Is it sparkling in the sunlight? Is it big and round? Is it filled with air? Now, let's put a word into the bubble. Put the word angry, or the feeling of being angry into your bubble. See the letters floating inside of your bubble or just see a color that means anger in your bubble. Do you see your letters? Do you see your color? Now give it a gentle tap with your hand. Push your bubble into the air. Do you see it bounce off of your hand? Now push it higher. There it goes. See it heading for the sky. Watch it go. You bubble is floating further and further away from you and it is taking your anger with it.

Anger Management Starts with You

If you were never given the skills as a child to handle anger in a healthy way then it makes sense that as an adult, you'd find this challenging. Maybe you lash out, or get weepy or withdrawn when faced with situations that make you angry. Or maybe you stuff your frustrations down until they resurface at an unexpected time. Either way, before you can constructively teach your children to cope with anger, you need to get a handle on how you express it so you can model good behavior.

As a parent, dealing with an angry child is inevitable and feared by all. Many of us have heard our own pre-parenting voice whisper to us, "That will never be my kid having a fit like that!"

How to Handle a Tantrum

You will learn quickly that meeting anger with anger never works and only escalates the situation at hand. Kids' temper tantrums and meltdowns are one of the most challenging and yes, embarrassing moments a mom or dad can face. They happen at the most inconvenient times and places. Temper tantrums are very different from a meltdown, but the way they make parents feel during the moment is the same. You may not be able to control or prevent your child from causing a scene, but you can always choose to stay centered, breathe, give your child space, but remain available. You can remain accountable for your own behavior and apply your newly acquired skill of responding instead of reacting.

Dr. Laura Markham, author of *Peaceful Parent, Happy Kids: How to Stop Yelling and Start Connecting* lends her insight. (*www .ahaparenting.com/*)

Your child needs you to witness her outpouring of emotion and let her know that she is still a good person, despite all these yucky feelings. So she needs your reassurance and permission. Explanations, negotiations, remorse, recriminations, analysis of why she's so upset, or attempts to "comfort" her (*"There, there, you don't have to cry, that's enough."*) will all shut down this natural emotive process. (Of course, you want to "teach"—but that needs to wait. Your child can't learn until she's calm.) You don't have to say much. Your calm, loving tone is what matters. Here's some language you could try:

> *You are so mad and sad.*
> *Go ahead and let it all out.*
> *We all need to cry sometimes.*
> *I hear how upset you are.*
> *I'll stay right here while you get all of your yucky feelings out.*
> *You're telling me you don't want me here, so I'll move away a little bit, but I am here for you.*
> *When you think you're ready, I'm right here to give you a hug.*

— Relax FAQ —

Q: My oldest daughter is 9 and can get very angry and start really kicking and hitting things, like her bed, stuffed animals, etc. Lately I have been just letting her get it out, but it doesn't seem healthy. Or is it? I want her to not suppress her emotions, but I also want her to have a healthy relationship with those emotions.

A: It sounds like your daughter is hurting or scared. Your most helpful response is compassionate empathy. Don't let her destroy property, or hurt anyone (including herself), and she shouldn't hurt her toys, but it's fine for her to lash out in that moment. You can stay calm and say, "Wow, you're so upset, what's going on?" She'll likely vent and tell you angrily what's wrong. Just listen, say "My goodness . . . No wonder you're upset . . ." Soon she'll get to the wound behind the anger. You can then hold her and empathize. The more you do this, the more quickly she'll get to the upset behind the anger, and the less she'll dwell on it. The anger is a wall around the heart to keep the pain out.

Imagine . . .
Close your eyes, take a deep breath, and imagine responding calmly and lovingly to your child's anger.

A Call for Help

Over and over again parents ask, "How do I punish my child out of this behavior?" The answer is simply: "You don't." You need to teach children into new behaviors, you cannot punish them out of undesirable ones. Take a deep breath and recognize that physical aggression is your child asking, "I need help from you in figuring out how to do this better." Assume when your child engages in acts of physical aggression, that she had no other choice available to her at the moment. She needs your support in finding better alternatives.

Parent's POV
On Discipline

"As parents, we need to work on emotional control. Parents who spank have merely lost their wits for a period of time. But we should call it what it is—bullying. There is always another option. Parents turn to spanking when they don't have a more creative way to get through to their child. Personally, I don't want my kids to see they can make me lose control of my emotions. I can also vouch for the research that says spanking doesn't do any good and can have harmful effects."—Catherine

A Word about Spanking

Spanking is an unhealthy expression of anger, frustration, and lack of self-control. Spanking makes children feel powerless and unloved. The theory of spanking relies on the thought that a child will stop the behavior to avoid another spanking. If this were accurate . . . spanking families would never have to spank.

Instead, parents can demonstrate healthy anger-management techniques that enable children to manage their own anger and frustration. Non-violent discipline provides opportunities to bond and connect with our children. Do your best to keep a positive outlook and always remember that raising children is filled with teaching moments.

MINDFUL MANTRA

Just for today, I will pause before I speak. I will be mindful to choose healing, loving, supporting words.

SANITY SAVER   Try keeping rose essential oil in your purse at all times. For centuries, rose fragrance has been used to help soothe people during periods of anger and grief.

Teaching Your Child to Express Anger

Here are several ways to do just that (adapted from a list created by UK parenting expert Elizabeth O'Shea, found at *www.parent4success.com*):

1. By modeling what we want them to do—such as taking time out when we are angry, asking assertively for what we want, and by finding an appropriate outlet for our physical energy.
2. Find an object that helps your child calm down. Some children will be comforted by a blanket, special soft toy, or soft cushion.
3. By having an area where they can go when they feel angry—and have materials to draw an angry picture, newspaper to rip up, bubble wrap to stamp on, a punch ball or pillow to punch, or a mini trampoline to jump on.
4. Ways of getting rid of pent-up angry energy can be running up and down the garden ten times or running up and down the stairs twenty times. A drum kit in the garage can also be very therapeutic!
5. Taking time out or a break can be a useful strategy, both for adults and children.
6. Some parents find holding, hugging, or rocking their child firmly helps the child feel safe when he is angry. (But do this with caution—an angry child can be quite violent, and some children may feel that physical restraint is a punishment and kick against you.)
7. Retreating to a quiet room may help. Reading a book to take his mind off the situation, or listening to relaxing music are all good choices. (Remember the relaxation oasis you created together.)
8. Alternatively, listening and dancing to high-energy music may be useful.

9. Playing with a pet, especially a dog, can help as children feel their pets are accepting. But don't suggest this strategy if you think your child may hurt the pet.

10. Teach them to explain how they feel assertively. Get them to fill in the blanks in the sentence "I feel . . . when . . . because . . . and I want . . ."

11. You can also ask your child what she finds helpful when she feels angry. If you give her time to think she may be able to suggest some great strategies of her own that work for her.

12. Finally, teach your child to problem solve. Have him write down a whole load of potential solutions to his problem. Add solutions of your own at the end and get him to choose which solutions he wants to try.

ᑫᑐ LORI'S LESSON ᕤᕐᑐ

Introducing children to simple self-soothing yoga poses is grounding and tangible. One of my favorite entry-level poses for kids is Child's Pose. It can pacify and comfort. For energy release and as a mood changer try Happy Baby Pose with your child. You and your inner child will thank you. Children can even be taught to use hand or finger mudras (yoga for the hands) to manage their energy during school or social situations when they feel overstimulated or angry.

Channeling Your Child's Angry Energy

Here are some very simple methods you can successfully use with young children to help diffuse a heated situation when they are angry. *(These are strategies you'll also find in more detail in my book,* The Angry Octopus.*)*

- Lie down for a rest.
- Tighten fists quietly and release.
- Find a quiet place.
- Talk it out. Give feelings words.
- Think about happy things.

- Breathe.
- Go for a walk.
- Take a break.
- Dance it off or exercise.
- Get into Child's Pose.
- Count backwards from ten.
- Take a bath and add rose petals for a playful twist.

Parent's POV
On Anger Management

"I have an 8-year-old daughter with serious anxiety problems. She practices these techniques and they help her feel better when she's having a bad day—it helps soothe her when she's mad or scared. She now uses the techniques on her own when she needs a quick calming down!"—Elizabeth

Mudras, arm exercises, and acupressure also present efficient ways for children to channel or diffuse their anger. A mudra can be as simple as pressing the thumb and index fingers together. Children gain an additional tactic when they find a hand position that can be used as a self-soothing tool. Mudras aren't just for yoga fans; even scientists are suggesting that crossing your arms over your midline can reduce pain. Here are some other exercises to try:

- Apply gentle downward pressure on the fleshy part of the ear lobe or cup the entire ear to create a sound that suggests the ocean.
- Apply upward thumb pressure to both inner corners of the eyebrows, just below the bone. This is effective and can be done in any public environment; it also works great with elbows on a desk making it an accessible tool to use in school or at work.

● Apply pressure or massage to the mid area of your forehead for instantaneous relaxation.

Children get more anxious, frustrated, and angry when they feel out of control of their own emotions, which also affects their self-esteem. When you give them solutions you show them that they are powerful. Just letting children know that they can find ways within themselves to self-regulate reduces anxiety and increases their self-esteem.

SANITY SAVER   Make wishes with your children. Take a deep breath, and make a dandelion wish or blow out a wish candle. Wishes are hope with a splash of magic: a playful way to reduce anger and keep your family optimistic.

PART III

STRESSFUL SITUATIONS, SOLVED

"We spend precious hours fearing the inevitable. It would be wise to use that time adoring our families, cherishing our friends, and living our lives."

—MAYA ANGELOU

CHAPTER 8

At School

"No one has yet realized the wealth of sympathy, the kindness and generosity hidden in the soul of a child. The effort of every true education should be to unlock that treasure."

—EMMA GOLDMAN

⚞ LORI'S LESSON ⚟

My 4-year-old daughter did not want to go to preschool. We had a two-block walk to school three days a week. She screamed the whole way. She was stressed-out and so was I. I knew there had to be a better way.

I addressed this issue of separation anxiety by role-playing. I asked a friend to play the role of the teacher and we turned her playhouse into a classroom. I walked my daughter to the playhouse door and handed her off to her teacher. We said goodbye and shut the door. I then opened the door a minute later saying I was returning to get her. Hugs, kisses, and celebrating what a good job she did going to school ensued. Each time, I added a few minutes to lengthen the separation time. The turning point was when I let my daughter pretend to be the mom while I took on the role of child. She brought me to the door. I resisted and protested that I didn't want to go. She reassured me that she would come back to get me! What a moment. We played this game throughout the weekend, using different rooms and scenarios. By Monday she no longer resisted going to school! We walked to school without crying and screaming. A little creativity and effort turned my anxiety-ridden child into a self-assured, more confident child.

With grade-school children spending more than 1,200 hours in the classroom each year and tasked with roughly four hours of nightly homework assignments (according to a University of Michigan study), it's no wonder today's kids feel stressed about going to school! When you throw in test taking and navigating the social landscape of school, including dealing with bullies, your main job as a parent could very well revolve around helping your little ones successfully go through these years while learning how to cope in the world. An incredible 70 percent of grade-school-age children admit that they worry—separation anxiety, sharing a teacher's attention with a group, making new friends, taking turns, and controlling impulses can all be exciting but stressful new learning experiences for children.

Parent's POV

On Starting the School Year

"We 'practice' getting ready for school every day for about a week before school starts. Then we go on an 'adventure' to get school supplies, to pick out lunch foods, after-school snacks, to the library, we drive the bus route, etc., then come home and talk about the most fun part. It helps channel the anxiety into excitement!" —Jennifer

Here are some general tips to help keep your child's back-to-school experience as stress free as possible:

- Accept the fact that all kids (no matter the age) will be cranky for the first two weeks back to school. Keep demands and schedules as light as possible until you and your child adjust to her new school schedule.
- Work through any of your own anxious feelings about back-to-school. Children pick up on spoken and unspoken anxiety. The more accepting you are about school, the more welcoming your kids will be.
- Never let your child hear you speak negatively about her teacher. Be positive and remember that a teacher who did not work well for your neighbor's child may turn out to be your child's favorite.
- If you know who will be in your child's upcoming class, use the summer break to introduce your child to at least one or two other children that will be in his class. If not, try to connect your child with one or two peers he would like to get to know better during the early weeks of school.

Children are especially sensitive to change. Acknowledge that any kind of change—negative *or* positive—creates stress. A little awareness coupled with creativity and compassion can make your back-to-school day stress free!

MINDFUL MANTRA

Just for today, I willingly accept the unknowns of the new school year. I embrace new opportunities and face change with a positive, relaxed attitude.

The true keys to living in harmony during the school year boil down to a few key tactics. If you are able to adopt even some of these in your home, you'll find that the stress-free days will outnumber the stressful ones and your child will begin to love his school days! Here they are:

Get on a schedule: Children respond positively to routine. Dry erase boards are great for writing the day's schedule. Kids love their own boards and feel less anxiety when they are aware of their schedule. Provide a variety of colors and watch your child step into this role of managing her schedule. (You may even want to consider turning an entire wall into a canvas; it's easily done with dry erase board paint.) Simply knowing when they have PE, and when they need to wear sneakers is helpful. Keep expectations age appropriate. Maintaining a consistent lights-out time will decrease bedtime resistance (more on reducing bedtime stress in the following chapter).

Limit your extracurricular activities: Be sure to pick sports and extracurricular activities that fit your family's lifestyle. For example, a team that demands three practices a week from 7:30 to 8:30 P.M. might not be worth the commitment—or lack of sleep for your child! Make sure you choose activities that create joy for your child, not stress.

Stay organized: This can be challenging, but even the simplest organization solutions can spare you lots of anxiety and chaos. Designate a shoe area; knowing where to find your child's shoes in the morning can eliminate crying and minutes wasted looking for them.

See what ideas your child has to streamline her morning routine and incorporate those into the mix. (*It was a great day when my kids decided to tie a hairbrush to the railing on the staircase. They have never again spent a morning rushing about, looking for a hairbrush.*)

Eat well and rest well: When your child is well rested she's also less irritable and better able to respond to stressful situations in a balanced, levelheaded manner. Nutrition is also important in this equation. Sugar, caffeine, and food coloring can increase the jitters and should be limited. A good balanced breakfast with protein can help your child start the day feeling centered. Non-traditional alternatives such as smoothies, protein bars, and even soup also work for breakfast.

Practice relaxation: Let your children see you taking a few minutes to sit still and concentrate on your breathing. Tell them what you are doing. Children copy what they see and don't be surprised if even your youngest child climbs up on your lap to experience belly breathing. Say your affirmations out loud and affirm your commitment to manifest a school year with less stress!

STRESS-LESS ACTIVITY: CELEBRATE LIFE

No birthdays or holidays needed. Simply bake some cupcakes or cookies with your children and throw a celebrate life party. Let the kids decorate and share an experience from your day where life showed you something that made you smile or feel grateful. Take turns sharing and throw a few "YIPPEES!" into the mix and watch the doldrums disappear. Sounds silly, but kids love silly and adults need silly.

School = Pressure Cooker

With an unprecedented amount of pressure to give your children the best education, it's easy to forget that your kids are incredible emotional, spiritual, social, and physical beings. Childhood (or school) should not be a stress-filled race to see who can read the most books, write the longest paper, and count to 100 in seven different languages! Childhood is a small window of time to learn, live, grow, and laugh with life. When you can allow children to develop at their own pace you ease their stress considerably.

Academics are obviously important, but it's also important to raise a healthy, balanced, whole person who will be able to find his or her own path and place in a world that so desperately needs more peacemakers, space explorers, healers, scientists, and storytellers. When you give your children the tools to manage stress and quiet the constant chatter in their minds, you clear space for them to see who they truly are. How many "straight-A" adults have sacrificed so much to be successful in a career that means nothing to them? Many still seek their life's purpose. How different would your life be if you grew up encouraged to explore your interests? What if you grew up in a relaxed way that gave you permission to follow your soul's purpose?

MINDFUL MANTRA

Just for today, I honor and support my child as he travels on this beautiful journey called life. I see him bright and full of hope; bursting with creativity and wellness.

Parent's POV
On Homework

"My son cannot do homework the minute he gets home. He has way too much pent up energy from all the pressures of the school day. I found that if I let him go out to play for one hour or more when we can, he can settle down, focus, and be more attentive to his assignment. I want to raise my children to not just cope, but cope well." —Cindy

SANITY SAVER   Create a designated area for your child's study space. Clear out the clutter and let him give it his own personal touch by displaying his artwork or an accomplishment he is proud of. An award, achievement certificate, or trophy can be inspirational when he has doubts about his abilities.

Teachers are underpaid, overworked, and entrusted with the most important job on the planet. They are put under enormous pressure to teach to standardized tests and perform within parameters of a school district's curriculum. A study published in the International Journal of Stress Management states that 67 percent of teachers surveyed described their jobs as extremely stressful. Teachers who were introduced to relaxation and breathing exercises reported significantly lower levels at the end of the year than teachers who did not participate in the program. Here's what Angela Brent-Harris, one enlightened grade-school teacher, had to say on the topic of homework and stress:

"As a first-grade teacher and mom, I allow my students to be themselves. I find that kids need to love themselves more and learn to treat others how they would like to be treated. I teach with love, compassion, and understanding. I believe that I set the steppingstones each year for my students so I create a nurturing environment—an environment without stress! My classroom is a sacred sanctuary. I allow no negativity to contaminate my class. Sometimes homework for a night will be to go home and fill a family member's bucket with love and kindness or just to give a hug. When kids are in my class, they leave with a priceless gift of self-esteem. This warms my heart. Again, this year I have a classroom full of nineteen happy, stress-free kids."

(Angela uses our Stress Free Kids® curriculum and has increased self-esteem for hundreds of children.)

Imagine . . .
Close your eyes, take a deep breath, and imagine what it would feel like to support your child from a place of knowing, affirming that your child is much more than her academic experience.

Taming Test Stress

Finals, a quiz, or standardized testing can evoke feelings of stress, fear, even panic. These strong emotions can affect your child's ability to think clearly and access information. It's normal for kids to feel a little nervous before a big test, but anxiety left unchecked can affect grades.

Here are some signs that your child is stressing or overly worried about tests. He or she:

- Doesn't want to go to school, especially on test day
- Cries or has meltdowns during the days leading up to a test
- Changes eating and sleeping patterns in the days before a test
- Puts herself down or calls himself "stupid"
- Has an upset stomach or a tension headache before a test
- Performs well on practice tests but not on the real test

Studies have shown that students who practice relaxation achieve higher test scores. You can help your children succeed when it comes to taking tests by introducing them to relaxation techniques. Deep breathing, visualizing, and repeating affirmations or positive statements will increase wellness—and increase grades.

Of these techniques, one of the most powerful stress-busters for test taking is positive self-talk. Anxiety can be lowered and confidence boosted with this simple technique. The following statements can be repeated before and during tests to mitigate stress:

- When stressed, I take deep slow breaths.
- I am calm, focused, and smart.
- I am relaxed and alert.
- I trust my knowledge.
- I know the answer to this question and I will look at it again in a few minutes.
- I am smart and relaxed.

- I remember to breathe deeply during my tests.
- Breathing deeply brings more oxygen to my brain.
- I have enough time to answer the questions.
- I have studied and I am prepared.
- Being calm helps me to remember more.
- I trust myself to do my best.

— Relax FAQ —

Q: How can I find out how my child is feeling about friends at school?

A: Schedule downtime for you and your child. If possible, carve out some time each day to connect with your child. Take a walk outside, or go out for dinner—just the two of you. Share a funny story about yourself when you were a child. These moments are relationship building and provide much-needed stress relief for you and your child! Ask specific questions like, "Who did you sit next to at lunch today?" "What games did you play at recess?" Unfortunately, parents are usually the last to know when their child is struggling socially. Children are usually too embarrassed to tell their parents that they are being excluded, teased, or bullied. But this bonding time can help give your child "permission" to open up, share her experiences, and ask for your help.

The new school year is *always* full of unknowns. You likely remember being afraid of getting the "mean" teacher . . . or having tension about sitting near the school bully. For many, school represented the first time you became aware of the sensations of stress, fear, and anxiety. That could largely be because of bullies.

Dealing with Bullies

Any child exposed to bullying on a physical or emotional level will experience an increase in stress levels. Even children that witness bullying are affected. It is important to identify stressors and realize that children are affected by stressful events like change or being excluded by their peers. Change in schedules, friendships, or trouble at school rate high as stressors for children. A schedule change from summer to school is enough to create feelings of stress and anxiety for some children. Couple that with early morning wake-ups, homework demands, and after-school activities and you have a recipe for stress. Now add complicated social situations as your children try to fit in at recess. Throw your own worries into the mix and you have entered a vicious cycle.

☞ LORI'S LESSON ☜

My young daughter arrived home from school crying as she explained that her feelings had been hurt by one of her friends. As the day progressed, she became increasingly sad and sick. By bedtime her stomach ached, she sobbed deeply, and she could not fall asleep. I realized that she needed to get the hurtful words out of her body and mind. We took a few deep belly breaths and imagined that she was blowing bubbles. Then we took the hurtful words and visualized putting the words into her bubble. We sent it way up high until it popped. My daughter closed her eyes and fell fast asleep with a smile on her face. I kissed her forehead and headed for my computer. I revisited a story I had begun writing ten years earlier called The Perfect Club. *Now I knew so much more about stress, anxiety, anger, and energy. I added coping strategies for each of the characters in this heartwarming story of acceptance and* Indigo Dreams: Garden of Wellness *was born.*

According to the National Association of School Psychologists, more than 160,000 children skip school every day because they feel threatened by another student. If you think your child is safe because he is not the class nerd and he can bounce a ball, think again. Many of the children being selected as victims are good-looking, athletic, smart, caring, and creative. Teachers are shocked when they hear this particular child is being bullied.

Parent's POV

On the Power of Relaxation Techniques

"I have three children ranging from 8 to 16 years old. They love to practice their deep breathing and positive affirmations. They especially find it very helpful during exams and also very useful when dealing with peer pressure in school. It gives them tools they can use to deal with the situation at hand in a positive, constructive manner, which aids in their self-esteem. I would highly recommend all parents teach this to their little ones!" —Angelo

Anxiety and self-esteem can either feed each other or rob each other of nutrients. Children struggling with stress are uncomfortable in their own skin. They feel out of balance. This constant uncertainty can lead to self-doubt. Self-doubt or low self-esteem affects a child's personality and how they interact with others. A child with compromised self-esteem will struggle with social interactions, which in turn creates more stress and possibly social anxiety. Self-value is bully repellent.

So, how can you help bully-proof your child? The best line of defense starts at home. Ask yourself the following questions:

- Do you bully yourself, beating yourself up for mistakes you make?
- Do you unknowingly bully your children? Do you over criticize them and correct everything they do?
- Does your spouse bully you? Do you treat each other disrespectfully?
- Do you accept bullying from your friends and remain in unbalanced or hurtful friendships?
- Do you forget to stand up for yourself?
- Do your children hear you participating in gossip?
- Do you ignore sibling rivalry that involves hitting, taunting, and teasing?
- Do you model any bullying behavior to your children, perhaps making plans to exclude others?

● Do you forget to set healthy boundaries, always saying yes to
everyone and everything?

If you have answered yes to the above questions be aware that
you may be unknowingly positioning your child to either be bullied
or become the bully.

The Anatomy of a Bully

The bully gains power while crushing another human being's spirit.
He (or she) increases his own self-value and satisfies his need to control others as he steals his victims' self-esteem rendering them with
feelings of worthlessness. But contrary to popular belief, the U.S.
Department of Health and Human Services states that children who
bully actually have an average to above-average self-esteem. This
changes the old belief that bullies have low self-esteem and don't like
themselves. Bullies are confident, have lots of friends, lack empathy,
and have a positive attitude towards violence. Any child with less
confidence and self-esteem than the bully becomes a potential tar-
get. Children that are bullied are facing a complicated multi-faceted
dilemma that most adults are unable to unravel. Teachers, psychologists, and bullying experts all argue their various methods on how to
stop bullying. Yet bullying incidents continue to rise.

This is the new face of bullying that is often hard to detect. There
are no visible bruises but the unseen emotional scars can ruin lives.
The levels and rules of bullying have changed and evolved. Raising
your children with a strong sense of self and value can help make
them less attractive to a bully. Families can set their intentions to
noticing the value in each other and build each other up with compliments that come from the heart—real compliments about their
personalities, not the meaningless type of overpraise you may have
become accustomed to. The following exercise will get you going in
the right direction.

STRESS-LESS ACTIVITY: CREATE COMPLIMENT BAGS

Give your kids a self-esteem boost and make a deposit in their self-value bank by creating family compliment bags.

Materials:

- Index cards folded in half horizontally (available in white, pastel, or neon)
- Brown or white paper lunch bags to decorate; colored gift bags are also fun
- Markers
- Crayons
- Glue
- Scraps of tissue paper, feathers, cutouts, etc., to glue onto bags

First have fun decorating a paper lunch bag (white is best). Fold index cards horizontally. Have each member of the family write a compliment inside of a folded index card with the name of the person to receive the compliment on the outside of card. Put each compliment in each other's bag. If children need help thinking of compliments, you can type up and print out a list of compliments they can choose from and glue onto the cards. Anytime your child is feeling like no one likes him, or hearing negative self-talk, he can reach into his bag and read his collection of compliments. Never underestimate the power of a heartfelt compliment.

Resilience Is Key

Izzy Kalman, a nationally certified school psychiatrist and author of *Bullies to Buddies: How to Turn Your Enemies Into Friends*, believes that we as a society are doing a lousy job of promoting resilience. "Rather than helping kids become people who can weather the slings and arrows of life, we are producing a generation of emotional marshmallows—kids who believe they are entitled to a life in which no one upsets them, and can't tolerate any insult to their minds and bodies." Raising children to be resilient is crucial in warding off a bully. The child that reacts emotionally distraught to a bully will only encourage the bully. So what can we do as parents to protect our children without turning them into marshmallows a bully will eat for dessert?

TIPS:
- Raise confident children based on inner belief, not false praise.
- Guide children, but allow them to handle normal playground conflicts.
- Socialize your children and seek social skills classes if needed.
- Expose your child to various groups and activities.
- Find groups or activities that support your child's uniqueness.
- Role-play laughing remarks off and creating comebacks.
- Introduce coping skills to release anger or hurt feelings.
- Empower children to manage anxiety.
- Maintain strong family connections with parents and siblings.
- Talk to your children about how they feel or the challenges they face.
- Help your child build relationships with peers by creating opportunities.
- Teach your children to smile and laugh at their mistakes.

It is important for you to observe your child with an objective eye. Notice the very things a bully would notice. Does your child walk with his head down? Does your child wear bright green fur socks? Does your daughter run over to you when the rest of the girls go to the break room? Does your son only sit with girls at lunch? You may feel as if the above examples are exactly what make your child oh-so-loveable . . . But many of these behaviors are a giant neon welcome sign to bullies. You do not have to discourage individuality and creativity, but be warned that it takes a strong and confident child to pull it off. So either make sure your child can rock those fuzzy green socks and stand up to teasing or leave them in the drawer for weekends!

CHAPTER 9

At Home

"What can you do to promote world peace? Go home and love your family."

—MOTHER TERESA

❧ LORI'S LESSON ❧

The main room or living room in my home is our family's relaxation oasis. It is free of clutter, has musical instruments on the coffee table and easy inspirational reading for adults, teens, and even children. TV and computers are noticeably absent and candles are always available. A fresh sprig of lavender or mint in a vase adds aromatherapy and brings the healing properties of nature inside. This is a place for connecting with other family members and supporting meaningful conversation. Mom, dad, and kids can sit back, find stillness, and let stress melt away. It is important for every home to have a sanctuary that nurtures your family's mind, body, and soul. Whether this is a shared space or an area just for you, it should be a place that allows you to withdraw from the chaos and clear your mind. My relaxation space reminds me to never underestimate the value of relaxation.

When it comes to creating a home environment that isn't mired in stress, you need to remember that it's often the small things that can make a big difference. While it may be too challenging to keep your entire home tidy and organized, you can commit to just keeping your dinner table or countertop free of clutter. You can have boundaries and routines in place that all contribute to a peaceful place that you are proud to call home—and allow your children to grow up without feeling undue chaos. This is the one area in your life you actually have some control over.

Working with Your Home's Energy to Create a Sanctuary

Of course, you will be the driver of how you organize and decorate your home, but your children can also participate in creating an environment that supports their own balance, good health, and happiness! Many decorators and holistic practitioners employ Feng Shui, an ancient Chinese practice of placement for enhanced energy flow. Believing in energy or Feng Shui is not a requirement. The point is to be playful and explore new ideas. In fact, many of you probably already do this innately. Every time you place an item on your mantel or move it a little to the left or a little to the right you are unconsciously working with Feng Shui.

⟳ LORI'S LESSON ⟳

My daughter wanted to hang a rainbow sun catcher in her room. Normally they are placed in front of a window, but she wasn't buying that idea. She was quite insistent on hanging it in a very specific corner of her room—far from any windows. Confused about her insistence, I opened my Feng Shui book to see if there was a deeper reason for why she wanted it placed there. She had placed it in what the Bagua map (a very basic tool used in Feng Shui to learn which parts of a space correlate with particular areas of life) referred to as the "Knowledge and Self-Cultivation" area. At the time, she was struggling with some new concepts in school. I started playing with this idea and drew up a Bagua map that she could relate to. We called it her knowledge and learning corner. She then further enhanced this corner of her room by adding her books and a comfortable pillow to sit on.

STRESS-LESS ACTIVITY:
USE A BAGUA MAP WITH YOUR CHILDREN

Trust your instinct and encourage your children to trust theirs when it comes to creating their very own peaceful bedroom space. They can use this Bagua map as a guide.

New Ideas & I can Do it	Dreams & Self Belief	Love & Friendship
Health & Family	Earth & Nature	Playing & Creating
Knowledge & Learning	Relaxing & Seeing Clearly	Giving & Accepting Help

Entrance
Your Door

©Copyright 2004 LoriLite

Let them paste hearts on the wall, or have a blanket that clashes with the pillowcases. Encourage them to choose colors that support their needs (e.g., What colors help make them feel relaxed? Happy? Which promote healing?). Give them the option to use holiday lights as a night-light. They could run a strand across a window frame or hang it down along a corner. They could also put glow-in-the-dark stars on the ceiling or soften the ceiling by tacking up material. Their imaginations should drive the exercise!

Imagine . . .
Close your eyes, take a deep breath, and imagine what it would feel like to step into a nurturing room that supports your peace of mind.

No matter how much of a sanctuary you make your home, there are inevitable times in which stress can still kick up with your children: mealtime, homework, and bedtime. Here's how you can achieve peace in all of these areas.

Peace at . . . Mealtimes

Children are notoriously picky eaters and this inevitably turns what should be a time to catch up with family into a stressful event. Luckily, there are steps you can take to make mealtimes more pleasant for everyone—and raise your children with healthy, open-minded eating habits.

Get your child involved. When you go to the grocery store or farmers' market, bring your child with you and ask for her help picking out items. You might even plan an outing to a local farm so that your family can learn firsthand where food comes from. When you're preparing meals, identify age-appropriate tasks they can help out with, such as putting salad into bowls or washing veggies. Kids will be proud of their contributions and more likely to eat the fruits of their labor.

Make one meal for the whole family. While it can be tempting to create multiple dishes so that you can serve both adult food and a kids' meal, it sends a message to your kids that they're not expected to make the same healthy choices that adults are. Cook one meal that includes at least one item you know your kids will eat and give up that second career of an at-home short-order cook!

Serve meals at the same time every night. When your family sits down to dinner at the same time every night, it expresses the importance of both eating and gathering as a family unit. Turn off the television and power down cell phones. Remove distractions and take the time to enjoy dinner *and* each other's company. Be flexible. If dinner togetherness doesn't work for your family, try a family breakfast routine.

Don't force a child to eat something he doesn't like. Don't get frustrated if your child doesn't want to try a healthy food right away. The more times your expose your child to broccoli, the better your chances are that he will decide to give it a try. Some studies suggest that this could mean ten to fifteen times! If your child is not willing to try a food, don't force him to eat it or make a big deal out of his refusal. Present other healthy alternatives and set that broccoli out on the table again and again as an option.

Give up membership to the clean-plate club. Present healthy, nourishing options at mealtimes, then let your child select what and how much of each food she eats. Rather than forcing a child to eat a certain amount, allow her hunger to dictate her serving sizes. This relaxed attitude eliminates unnecessary power struggles.

Don't use food as a bribe. When you reward a child with a dessert after he eats all of his vegetables, you reinforce the belief that healthy foods are something to suffer through so he can get to the "good stuff" (i.e., sugary sweets). Treat foods neutrally, instead, and you may find that your child enjoys homemade applesauce sweetened with honey more than a sundae with storebought chocolate syrup.

Share a meal and a story. When you share healthy meals with your children, tell them how much you're enjoying the roasted vegetables or apple slices on your plate. If you used to hate Brussels sprouts when you were younger, but now you love them roasted with a little bit of olive oil, share that story! This will open their minds to the possibility of one day enjoying a food they didn't think they would ever appreciate. Your child will delight in knowing that you, too, have made some dietary adjustments based on your evolving taste buds.

Parent's POV
On Dinnertime

"Dinnertime is always chaotic at my house. The kids resist eating most of their dinner and I find myself constantly getting up from the table to make them their staple macaroni and cheese. I am tired of feeling like a waitress and a server. I want to sit down and eat a full meal without interruption." —Karen

✺ LORI'S LESSON ✺

When my kids came home from school they'd always storm the snack pantry, so I decided to capitalize on their ferocious appetites and serve a full meal as soon as they got off the bus. I personally enjoyed joining them to eat a larger meal at this time of the day. Since Dad worked from home, he was often able to accompany us. On the days he was unavailable, the kids had a chance for a double dose of table time as they could join Dad to talk about their day when Dad ate his dinner later in the evening.

Studies suggest that families that eat dinner together are more likely to eat healthier, suffer less from depression, and do better in school. A 2011 Columbia University study even shows that children who regularly eat dinner with their families are less likely to smoke, drink, or use drugs. This simple act of parental engagement can yield benefits that go beyond the expected.

STRESS-LESS ACTIVITY: DINNER CONVERSATION PROMPTS

Need a conversation starter at mealtime that all ages can embrace? Open a children's thesaurus and let each family member pick a word that the others need to give interchangeable words for. This increases vocabulary and gets everyone talking.

SANITY SAVER   Display a weekly or daily menu of meals on a chalkboard in the kitchen. Let kids take turns selecting one staple food you know they'll eat to be included with the meal. The rest is mom's pick.

Peace with . . . Homework

Just say the word *homework* to a child or parent and watch them go into stress mode. Homework stress can be reduced to transform homework hour into a positive experience that teaches your child life-long skills. When homework is too extensive and time-consuming it can have a negative impact on your overall effort to achieve balance. Take a good look at your child's homework routine. If your child ends up crying, sleep deprived, or quitting activities to have more time to complete assignments he may be experiencing stress overload.

This is shockingly common. Sixty-five percent of students report they are often or always stressed by their schoolwork and homework. Homework is a significant cause of stress for students! Homework can cause children to experience stress-related symptoms such as headaches, difficulty sleeping, exhaustion, and weight gain. When students perceive homework as a useful learning experience, they report fewer academic worries, fewer stress-related physical symptoms, and more positive mental health. A little awareness and a few tips can turn your child's homework into a positive, stress-free experience.

Designate a study area: Set up an area in your home dedicated to homework and studying. An area clear of chaos and with good lighting makes it easier for children to focus and feel at ease. Make sure it's free of clutter and items that can distract children. While you want to make this space available, be flexible and understand that your child may thrive by changing locations. Either way, it is nice to know they can return to the clutter free workspace when needed.

Purchase a second set of books: Purchase a second set of used textbooks to keep at home. This is especially helpful for children that have difficulty juggling assignments and organizing. It is also a healthy choice for your child's spine. Online shopping on Amazon.com makes it easy and affordable. Or, download the electronic version and get the added bonus of a lighter book bag.

Set smaller obtainable goals: Break it down. Set smaller goals to complete a portion of the assignment. Reward your child with a break. Let your child set a timer to alert him that his break is over. Listen to your child's input to decipher what amount of time results in optimal concentration. This eliminates power struggles and gets your child invested in supporting his own needs.

Celebrate small accomplishments: Brain breaks should be taken. Blow bubbles outside in the fresh air. Do jumping jacks, run, or have a good laugh. Exercising and deep breathing brings refreshing oxygen to your child's brain.

Encourage emotional intelligence: Some children need absolute quiet when concentrating while others do really well while listening to background relaxation music. Children participate in their own emotional awareness when they realize which environments contribute to their ability to study.

Provide guidance: Encourage children to review work each night so that when it is time for a test they are not overloaded with information. Help your child understand directions, organize, and create a time-management plan. Many children have no concept of time-management and lack the ability to plan ahead.

Strive for nutritional balance: Give your child a healthy snack or even a meal before homework. It is difficult for anyone to concentrate, sit still, or remain alert when hungry.

Incorporate stress-management techniques: Teach children relaxation techniques. Encourage them to take a deep breath in and say *"Ahhhhh"* to release anger and frustration. Stress gets in the way of learning and clear thinking. Learning, memory, concentration, and the ability to recall and access information can be affected.

Stay positive: Stay positive about and during homework. Your positive attitude enhances your child's mood. Do not complain about the teacher or the assignment. This only adds negativity and fear to your child's already full plate.

Even with taking steps to alleviate stress, experts warn that difficult homework assignments and the pressure to complete multiple projects can cause anxiety, frustration, and even anger for kids. Homework that creates an anxiety-ridden child is defeating the overall goal of creating a well-rounded, balanced, successful child. As a parent, you have the right to step in and get involved if you see this happening to your child. Be an advocate for your child. If she is overwhelmed by homework and it is affecting her quality of life, speak up. Teachers want to work with parents as a team. Your child's teacher will appreciate your honesty and availability.

Peace at . . . Bedtime

A study out of Tel Aviv University found that a mere one hour of missed sleep can reduce a child's cognitive abilities by two years! Getting children to bed can be a maddening experience for parents and kids. However, you can break any bad habits that persist by introducing strong bedtime boundaries and setting the stage for sleep with these relaxing routines.

STRESS-LESS ACTIVITY: CREATE A KID SPA

Turn bathtub time into relaxing spa time by letting your child play with a cup filled with baking soda. It is inexpensive and fully dissolves in the water, while softening and soothing skin. It amps up the alkalinity of the water and is said to aid in detoxifying. The silky water creates a luxurious feel that even kids can't resist.

⮜ LORI'S LESSON ⮞

One of my children loved to sleep with us. After waking up with one too many stiff necks and bruises from little legs kicking blankets off, we decided it was time to reclaim our mattress. I worked with my child to set her up with her own sleeping spot on the floor at the bottom of our bed. (A sleeping bag assured that it would not be too comfy.) Then, we set up a point system for her as an incentive to sleep in her own bed. We found a clear container and one small pompom went in for choosing to go into her sleeping bag without waking up mom and dad. Two bigger pompoms were added when she stayed in her own bed for the entire night. After three nights of point collecting, the container was filled and we were able to celebrate with a trip to the park. In a few weeks, my daughter grew tired of sleeping on the floor and her bed became her sanctuary.

SANITY SAVER   Many children become disinterested or bored with point systems. Jazz it up by changing out the actual point item. Initiate an outing to the Dollar Store and let kids select seasonal items to keep it entertaining. Even hair barrettes or plastic spiders can be used for points.

MINDFUL MANTRA
Just for today, I will focus on transforming bedtime into a peaceful, restful, bonding experience.

Snooze or Lose

Mary Carskadon, PhD, former president of the Sleep Research Society says it best: "Sleep is the forgotten country and is not getting the attention it merits. It plays out in the home, in the pediatrician's office, and in school. Sleep is an important factor in the lives of children."

One of the most stressful and common problems that parents and kids face today is bedtime. Most parents say that they would like to improve their child's bedtime routine. Here are a few simple tips that can make your bedtime routine stress free and dissolve your bedtime problems.

Focus on relaxation: One thing you can do to make bedtime stress free is focus on relaxation instead of the actual act of falling asleep. And you can encourage relaxation by exploring the use of aromatherapy and eye pillows. Eye pillows are soothing and also encourage children to keep their eyes closed. Eye pillows filled with flax seed have the added benefit of providing just the right amount of pressure to relieve tension. Your child's eyes, eyebrows, and temples will receive a little "hug." A few minutes of massaging your child's back, hands, feet, or even scalp can knock an hour off of his bedtime routine.

Set the mood: It's important to make the whole energy of the house settle down before bedtime. Dim the lights, lower the volume, shut off the TV, and restrict stimulating video games before bedtime. If you have older children in the house, it's especially important because the younger children feel the "awakeness" and the energy of the older kids and it's very hard to get the younger children to settle down. Have the family work together as a team to dial down the intensity and contribute to the common goal of simmering down. Everyone will benefit.

Create a peaceful space: Paint your child's room a soothing color. Bright reds and oranges are more active colors, while light blues, greens, and tans are more tranquil. Let your children participate in the color selection by offering them a palette of soothing colors that help them to feel peaceful and safe.

Improve relationships: With a little effort, you can turn bedtime into an unhurried, pleasant, bonding experience that actually enhances your relationship with your child, yourself, and your spouse. What's more is that you'll find extra time for yourself at the end of the day—that's always a treat.

SANITY SAVER   If you feel as if your kids are sleep-deprived, you're not alone. A survey by KidsHealth.org found that 70 percent of kids said they wished they could get more sleep and 71 percent of kids said they felt sort of sleepy or very sleepy when it's time to wake up for school. Your commitment to get your kids to bed early means you are perfectly sane!

ℰ LORI'S LESSON ℘

*I spent two hours every night trying to get my son to go to sleep. The more I focused on getting him to sleep the more determined he became to stay awake. He would empty out his dresser drawers, decorate his room with hangers, build forts in his closet, jump on the bed, and even managed to give himself a haircut. I was exhausted, stressed, and angry having to deal with this at the end of a long day. I began to create bedtime stories that not only entertained my son, but at the same time incorporated an actual relaxation technique. My son followed along and fell asleep. (*The Goodnight Caterpillar *story helps kids to unwind.)*

YOUR BEDTIME CHEAT SHEET:

- Take distractions out of the room.
- Focus on relaxing.
- Paint the room in soothing colors.
- Bring the energy of the whole house down a notch. Dim lights, use soft voices, lower radio or TV volume, or turn screens off completely.
- Give foot massages.
- Avoid reading stimulating, exciting, or scary stories.

STRESS-LESS ACTIVITY: SWEET DREAMS

Try combining massage, acupressure, and aromatherapy. Place a drop of lavender essential oil on your finger and massage the center of your child's forehead in a circular motion. If your child is sensitive to oils, you can opt to place a drop on a cotton ball and place in a nearby corner of the room. Involve your child by referring to this as their sweet dreams massage.

❧ LORI'S LESSON ❧

My 8-year-old daughter introduced us to stress-related night terrors. Her screams would jolt us out of bed to find her running through the house in a state of complete unawareness. We responded by remaining calm and allowing the process to unfold with an eye toward keeping her safe. In a few minutes, we could gently guide her back to bed. We took a close look at her stressors and discovered that her seat had been changed at school, with the hope that her rule-abiding, agreeable demeanor would rub off on a boy in class who repeatedly acted out. We asked the teacher to relocate her back to her original seat. When her seat was changed back, the night terrors evaporated as quickly as they had appeared. Case solved.

—— Relax FAQ ——

Q: How much sleep should my child be getting each night?

A: According to the National Sleep Foundation, grade-school-aged children should get anywhere from 10–13 hours of sleep a night, with younger kids logging more hours and older kids logging fewer hours. For 5- to 12- year-olds, 10–11 hours of sleep is recommended for optimum sleep benefits. Of course, every child is different and you will quickly learn how much sleep makes your child better able to tolerate the demands of his schedule.

SANITY SAVER   Don't think that your child purposely waits until "lights out" to let you know about all of her aches and pains. Dr. Heather Manley, author of the Human Body Detectives series, points out that this occurs because cortisol levels are lower at night, which in turn makes the body more sensitive to pain.

Older children can soothe growing pains or muscle aches by curling up to a microwaveable heat-pack. Earth Therapeutics has relaxing comfort wraps that are filled with rice and their special blend of lavender, chamomile, and citrus. The removable cover is machine washable.

CHAPTER 10

At Play

*"It may be that all games are silly.
But then, so are humans."*

—ROBERT LYND

ᘓᘔ LORI'S LESSON ᘒᘓ

My son wanted to connect with children in his new class. I scheduled play-dates that involved an activity instead of just coming over to play. Meeting at Chuck E. Cheese's, going to the movies, fishing, or visiting the zoo gave my son a chance to have one-on-one bonding time that carried over into the group setting. Boys especially benefit from being given a "doing something" activity they can then create conversation around. They will talk about winning 100 tickets at the arcade, or the bugs they found in the park, or the fish they caught at the pond, giving them a jumping off point of interacting when they are in a social situation.

> *Imagine . . .*
> Close your eyes, take a deep breath, and imagine what it feels like to be an observer of your child playing, laughing, and making friends.

My colleague, Ava Parnass is an author, songwriter, and child therapist who specializes in marrying entertainment and social-emotional literacy for kids. You can find her online at *http://listentomeplease.com/*. In this chapter, she shares her ideas for why play is so important and provides practical tips for how you can defuse stressful playdate situations.

Make Time for Play Time

There's an old saying: "A child's job is to play" and as parents, it's your job to ensure that your children participate joyfully in this essential part of childhood development. This generation is experiencing an increase in technology, texting, homework, and two parents working in addition to a decrease in recess time. As such, educators, child therapists, and parents need to come together to ensure kids don't lose an extremely important aspect of their childhood and continue to get enough unstructured playtime.

Play gives you a window into your child's emotional world. Play helps you appreciate your child's unique personality and builds closeness, connection, love, joy, and emotional intelligence. In addition, play decreases stress by allowing children to work through tough situations.

Play sets the stage for a lifetime of communicating effectively, listening, successful intimate relationships, developing trust, and learning how to get emotional and physical needs met.

Playdate Difficulties, Deciphered

Child #1: Says to your child, "You are weird!"

Child #2: Remains quiet but face looks very hurt and starts crying.

Child #1: "You really are weird!"

Parent: As you give a quick hug to the hurt child and say, "I am sorry your feelings are hurt." (Ask the other child,) "I'm wondering what did you mean to say?"

Child #1: "I don't know."

Parent: "Did something hurt your feelings? Because 'weird' is a hurtful word to use."

Child #1: "I didn't like that she said I was taking too long."

Parent: "Okay, so can you tell her that your feelings were hurt instead of using a hurtful word back?"

Results: The kids were able to talk it out.

Child #1: "You're a weirdo!"

Child #2: "I'm not playing with you."

Child #1: "I'm not playing with YOU. I want to go home!"

Parent: "Sounds like some feelings are hurt here, let's figure out what you really meant to say!"

Child #1: "I don't know."

Parent: "Did you get scared by his new idea? Did you mean to say, 'That's interesting,' 'Let me think about it,' or 'That's scary'?"

> **Child #1:** "Yes it was interesting but it was a different idea. Maybe it did scare me, what if I can't play that?"
> **Child #2:** "I can show you how and it's just for fun."
> **Child #1:** "Okay. Let's try it."
> *Result (from Child #1): "It was new but I liked it! You have interesting ideas!"*

Become a "Behavior-Feelings Detective"

Play helps you model emotional intelligence skills for your child. Teaching these skills is important so your child can then begin to understand and express her inner world—and in turn this decreases her stress levels.

For example, sometimes when children say they don't want to play with a particular friend, they are communicating some sort of hurt feelings. It is our job as parents to figure out what it means by teaching new words, new feelings, and new behaviors. Research shows that kids who play pretend and learn emotional intelligence skills early in life do better in all areas and are happier and more successful.

STRESS-LESS ACTIVITY: CARD GAMES

Dealing, shuffling, and holding cards in your hands may sound old-school, but with children spending so much time playing games like Solitaire online, a deck of cards provides a counterbalance. There is so much to learn from an old-fashioned card game: reading, counting, taking turns, manual dexterity, strategies, and communicating or working with another person. Grandparents often feel at a loss on how to interact with their technology savvy grandchildren. A card game puts everyone at ease and gets grandparents back in the game. I bet Pop can even teach the kids a card trick or two.

How to Become a Playful Grownup

When you are a playful grownup, your home becomes a place kids love coming to. When your child's friend visits, spend a few minutes talking to them and making them feel welcome. Have snacks on hand or find out ahead of time what types of food they like. Set up one room that is the free play area and give them space to be creative. Some ideas for creative play props include keeping a fold-away trampoline, a swing chair if you are adventurous, a chalkboard, or a karaoke machine. Comfortable bean bag chairs, brightly colored throw pillows, and a child friendly area where kids can be kids creates a warm and inviting feeling. An easy access basket full of crayons, stuffed animals, Qubits, or Legos can be an icebreaker. If your kids and their friends find comfort, fun, and acceptance in your home they will be more likely to enjoy their visit. If playdate troubles arise they will feel safe approaching you and asking for your advice.

Parent's POV
On Child Play

"I remember my friend's mom's basement with a hopscotch board painted on the floor. It was a great place to hang out. Her mom was very cool. I remember her having an avid interest in all of our lives. Having adults in your life that care that much means a lot."
—Theresa

How to Play and Listen Effectively

It's a myth that your child doesn't want to play with you or talk to you. They love it! It's just a matter of how you play, and how effectively you listen. You must work the fine line between being a parent who sets limits, being a playful grownup who knows how to have fun, and being available as a confidant. You need to strike a balance between allowing them time with their friends, and time with you. With a little awareness, you can create a safe place where children feel loved, valued, and listened to.

If you want your children to communicate with you, be the parent that listens when they speak. (Remember that having a communicative relationship is your responsibility, not your child's.)

Here are a few ways that you can communicate you are available and listening:

- Move away from your computer.
- Make eye contact.
- Sit beside your child.
- Respond thoughtfully.
- Acknowledge their feelings.
- Hold hands.

To curb stress that can often accompany playtime, listen well, use empathy, use your imagination, have patience, and go with the flow of pretend. Here are a few tips from Ava Parnass, (fondly known as @listentomepleas on Twitter) to keep in your pocket:

1. **Establish a routine.** At the beginning of playdates ask each of the children to tell you what they liked about their day as well as what they didn't like. Respond with empathy: "Thanks for telling me," "That was interesting," or "I'm sorry that happened, that sounds hard."
2. **Smooth the way.** Invite kids over who may not be getting along and present them with a creative project they can work on together to bond, for example, make a movie, or write a story or song.
3. **Ban technology.** Make your house an "old-school" interactive house and do not use the computer or phones during playtime. (This goes for adults, too!)

4. **Establish a healthy house.** Always remember that healthy snacks = healthy feelings. Serve love, fun, feelings, water, and fruits, but NO soda, juice, or junk food.

5. **Challenge children to make up games.** Ask kids what game they want to play, or make suggestions. If you want to be in their life, don't control their play by scolding or making excessive demands. If they start asking you to leave the room so they can play freely at an early age, it's a clue that you're being overly controlling.

SANITY SAVER   If your child doesn't seem to be a natural at socializing, don't worry. Social skills vary and can be learned through practice, guidance, and providing lots of opportunities.

Parent's POV
On Enthusiastic Play

"I poignantly remember a playdate of riding bikes in the freezing NYC cold when the kids decided that they were wild white horses in a race. I had to be the announcer and judge the race, rainbow horses against the white stallions. Each time they won I had to give them pretend oats to eat, which was Brothers-All-Natural Fruit Crisps. To me that was a win-win activity: exercise, fun, adults and kids playing together, healthy snacks, and imagination at work. My favorite type of play day!" —Ava

MINDFUL MANTRA

Just for today, I will give my children the space they need to explore their personalities and their friendships.

CHAPTER 11

In Sports

*"A trophy carries dust.
Memories last forever."*

—MARY LOU RETTON

✎ LORI'S LESSON ✑

I signed my daughter up for competitive cheerleading so that she could make new friends, be involved with a coach she could look up to as a mentor, experience the collective energy of belonging to a team, and improve her self-esteem. Cheerleading met these needs and more—it added joy and value to both of our lives. However, two years later, a new coach stepped in. This coach degraded and called the girls names, got drunk at an away competition, and expressed his anger by putting his fist through a gym-sized mirror. What started out as a positive experience that met our needs, became a negative, toxic, and dangerous environment. I was shocked that I was the only parent in the group that felt this detrimental situation outweighed the benefits of the activity.

When it comes to your child's involvement in sports, it's important to remember that it should positively add to your child's quality of life—as well as your own. If the activity makes your child miss out on needed sleep, feel miserable, or gets in the way of homework, you need to reevaluate whether it's worth staying involved with the sport. If you are feeling resentful about your child's demanding sports schedule, something needs to change. Don't be afraid to try something different and stand up for your values.

—— Relax FAQ ——

Q: How do I know which sport is right for my child?

A: Every child has different needs. Your son might enjoy baseball while your daughter enjoys tennis. Honor your children by letting them try various sports and see which one brings a sense of joy and accomplishment to their lives. You'll need to closely observe whether they feel energized by a particular sport or whether it depletes them. If it's the latter, it'll likely lead to stress. Sometimes, children don't want to continue playing a sport but don't know how to break the news to you. So be sure to ask if your child really *wants* to play the sport or if he's just doing it to please you or someone else. Enthusiasm is hard to fake.

My colleague, Jeff Botch, is a little league coach and author of the children's book, *Big Feats*. You can find him online at *www.jbotchbooks.blogspot.com* or on Twitter at @jeffbotch. In this chapter, he shows how you can introduce your child to sports without also introducing stress.

Sports give children the opportunity to be active, to interact with others their own age, to learn how to win and lose gracefully, and to develop themselves for the purpose of succeeding at improving. Sports help build your child's confidence, social skills, and begin to give her a sense of community. And sports also represent a wonderful way to introduce your child to a way to learn discipline. But regardless of the sport or league your child plays in, you need to always remember: It's about FUN.

A Sport for Every Child?

Even if a child isn't a natural athlete, it is still important that he has something he feels he's good at and can have fun doing. Here are a few suggestions to help engage your children if they are not certain what they want to play:

Watch a televised sporting event together . . .

- Ask them if they have friends that play this sport.
- Ask them which team they want to win.
- Ask them if they have played this sport at school or ever wanted to play.
- Ask them if they could picture themselves playing this sport.

Become active with your child . . .

- Invite your child to go outside and learn to play a sport with you. Keep it simple, play catch, kick the ball, or hit a tennis ball against the garage. This is a great opportunity to do something together as it encourages activity and at the same time will boost your child's self-esteem.

Go to a local sporting event together . . .

● This is another wonderful opportunity to spend quality time with your children and teach them about the game. Tell them about the players that you grew up watching and some of the memorable moments that impacted you when you were their age. Children like to model their parents and they will be more likely to want to play if they know you love the sport or played it when you were a child.

Watch other kids playing the sport . . .

● Go to your local ball field and watch other boys and girls their age playing.

● Let them know how easy it would be to participate, if they choose to play.

● Don't forget to grab a snack at concessions and make it as memorable as possible!

Once your child begins to take part in a certain game or sport, you will be able to sense how much she is actually enjoying it. With the proper coaching, along with encouragement and support from you and your whole family, your child will begin to see her potential, which gives her a green light to let her take it to the level that she is enthusiastic about.

> ### Parent's POV
> #### On the Good Influence of Sports
> "I've seen my previously klutzy child become more coordinated and really engaged as a result of taking gymnastic lessons. She looks forward to it every week and has even started to make friends with the other girls in her class. I'm so grateful for this positive influence in her life." —Abby

Adding the activity of a sport to a child's routine can have many positive benefits. As you know, it is nice to have something to look forward to after a busy day at work, or in the child's case, following a long day at school. Looking forward to soccer practice, a baseball game, or dance class will afford your child an outlet to focus on something else. It will also help them to develop friends outside of school.

Many children would opt for watching nonproductive television shows and playing video games over participating in an activity that gives them the chance to exercise, meet new people, and develop themselves. Parents have an obligation to steer their kids in the direction that gives them the greatest opportunity to develop the skills needed to manage their emotions and create future success. Playing sports provides them with the opportunity to develop these much-needed skills along with promoting a positive self-esteem, which greatly assists in lowering the stress associated with being a kid.

So Many Sports, So Little Time . . .

But what happens when your family's sports rotation begins to take over your life? (After all, you're a parent, not a chauffeur!) Between practices, fundraisers, scrimmage games, regular season games and matches, and playoffs or post-season competitions, youth sports schedules can cause even the most organized parent to become unhinged. Here are five tips to help you retain a sense of balance:

1. Commit to only one sport each season.
2. Gather and organize all necessary equipment so that it's ready beforehand.
3. Plan meals ahead of time and avoid the fast-food line. Slow cooker meals or soups work wonders on game days.
4. Reframe the experience. Instead of saying, "I have to take my kid to practice" say, "I am grateful I can take my child to practice."

5. Allow yourself to miss a practice or game once in a while; you can't always be there.

Above all, let children know your love for them is not based on their athletic performance.

SANITY SAVER Arrange for your kids to carpool with other families or take turns with your spouse, for times during the busy sports season when you can't be in two places at once! Your child will understand if you can't make every game, especially if you make a point of attending the majority of them and ask lots of questions about the games, meets, or matches that you can't attend.

ℰↃ LORI'S LESSON ℱↄ

My friend's son told his dentist that he was not the athletic type. We need to be careful not to impress our own expectations and definitions of athleticism onto our children. This self-defined non-athletic boy may not be on the football team, but he is well on his path of becoming a black belt in karate . . . Sounds pretty athletic to me.

Imagine . . .
Close your eyes, take a deep breath, and imagine what it would feel like to have your child involved in a sport that builds his confidence and allows him to thrive.

By now, we can all agree that one of the most effective ways for children to release everyday stress is to participate in athletics. After all, growing up is not an easy task and the stress that goes along with being a child can be immense.

STRESS-LESS ACTIVITY: BREATHING OUT THE JITTERS

Some pre-game jitters are healthy and can help your child perform at his peak. Many great athletes, including tennis great Martina Navratilova, employ breathing techniques to increase their stamina and endurance.

1. Breathe in, 2, 3, 4, and out, 2, 3, 4.
2. Breathe in great tennis and out great tennis.
3. Breathe in good sportsmanship and out good sportsmanship.
4. Breathe in confident catching and out confident catching.
5. Breathe in having fun and out having fun.

Substitute the word to meet your child's needs or just have your child repeat a word that helps him to regain his composure. "Calm, calm, calm." Taking deep breaths reduces jitters, increases endurance, and brings more oxygen to moving muscles.

A Word about Concussions

There's been a lot of talk in the news lately about concussions and it's about time. The CDC reports that more than 50 percent of all head injuries go unreported. There are approximately 173,000 cases of traumatic brain injuries in young athletes under the age of 19 each year.

This is all too common in today's sports and something you need to be aware of if your children are participating in sports, as it could have long-term health consequences that go way beyond the effects of stress.

—— **Relax FAQ** ——

Q: What is a concussion?

A: A concussion is a type of traumatic brain injury caused by a bump, blow, or jolt to the head or by a hit to the body that causes the head and brain to move rapidly back and forth. While most athletes recover quickly and fully from a concussion, some will have symptoms that last for days, or even weeks. A more serious concussion can last for months or longer.

As a conscientious parent of a young athlete, here's what you need to know about traumatic brain injuries:

Know the signs and symptoms. Read all the latest information on the CDC Heads Up site, *www.cdc.gov/concussion/headsup*. Talk with your coaches, athletic trainers, players, and others in the sports community about your findings. The more eyes on the game the better the chances of catching possible injuries.

Team up with others. Get together with coaches, parents, anyone involved in the athletic department to design a concussion action plan, if they don't already have one. Provide resources for everyone to read about the signs and symptoms of a concussion. The more involved, the better the outcomes.

Educate your child on when to sit it out. The overwhelming message in sports has been "Be tough! Shake it off!" Your child needs to know that it is all right to sit out a game or two if he doesn't feel right. Especially if he's recovering from a hard hit to the head, sitting out is mandatory.

Know the laws. The Zackery Lystedt Law was created to protect young athletes, and it is being passed in many states. Check to see if your state has approved it and if your athletic department adheres to the regulations.

When in doubt, seek medical attention. If you suspect a possible head injury, don't hesitate to seek medical attention. You can't be too careful when it comes to a head injury.

MINDFUL MANTRA

Just for today, I will be a responsible parent, monitoring
my child's well-being while realizing that win or lose,
my child is gaining valuable life lessons.

CHAPTER 12

When Traveling

*"In America there are two classes of travel—
first class, and with children."*

—ROBERT BENCHLEY

❧ LORI'S LESSON ❧

My daughter started to scream when airport security took her stroller and her blanket to scan it through the screening machine. It didn't help that her brother was telling her the scanning machine was a blankie-eating monster. It was quite entertaining for the passengers, but not for us.

> *Imagine . . .*
> Close your eyes, take a deep breath, and imagine what it would feel like to leave extra time to pack and leave the house feeling organized as you begin your journey.

Traveling brings on a host of stressors for kids: the unknown, change in schedule, rushing, strangers, fast-moving crowds, sensory overload, and less-than-healthy food choices. Here, you'll learn how to get through these times with ease and grace.

STRESS-LESS ACTIVITY: ASSIGN A TRAVEL BUDDY

You can transform traveling through airports by letting your children choose and take a travel buddy with them. A favorite doll or stuffed animal can help to eliminate fear and ease anxiety. Explain exactly what their travel buddy will experience during the trip. This introduces children to your travel plan and addresses any fears of the unknown. For added impact, play airport with your child and her travel buddy. You can wait in line, walk through your "doorway" metal detector, and buckle in. Practice handing the travel buddy to someone else and getting it back as you might have to do during security checks. A little playful investment at home can set your intentions for a smooth trip.

Air Travel Tips to Eliminate Stress for Kids and Parents

Nothing is worse than realizing that the screaming child on the plane is your own! The restrictive space and criticizing eyes of other passengers put parents at an extreme disadvantage. Most children realize that you will most likely not discipline them in public. So how can you avoid this challenge and set yourself up for a stress-free trip?

- Pack an activity bag. A great addition to it is Crayola Model Magic modeling compound. Bring a few different colors but only give your child one color at a time. Whenever he grows tired of the color surprise him with another color. Bring a few sculpting tools like a plastic fork, spoon, or Q-tips. Don't be surprised if the adult passengers want to join in on the fun. (Even young children enjoy watching their parents work the clay.)
- Allow more time than usual for traveling. It is impossible to feel easygoing when you are rushing about and a rushed child is often a screaming child.
- Pack healthy snacks and drinks. Most airlines no longer offer meals or anything more than peanuts and pretzels. A hungry or thirsty child is usually a crying child. Leave time to purchase beverages after clearing through security.
- A laptop or tablet with a movie and headphones is a great way to keep kids entertained on a plane.
- Bring along relaxation tracks or classical music. The best scenario is a sleeping child until you land!
- Carry an extra set of clothing.
- Let children have their own small carry-on backpack or rolling bag. Kids gain a sense of independence when they are in charge of packing it and carrying it. It also gives them something to focus on and keeps them involved in the process.
- Children are more apt to cry during takeoff and landing. Have gum or hard candy to share with your child for takeoff and landing. The sucking action will help them clear their ears.
- A pacifier can work wonders for clearing ears. If need be, place a bit of sugar on it to encourage sucking during takeoff and landing. Older children can create the same effect with a lollipop.

(Note: I am not normally a sugar fan but desperate plane ride moments call for this trick.)

- Children can be taught simple relaxation techniques ahead of time. Children that know how to focus on their breath as they breathe in and out can employ this technique on the plane. Even the youngest will settle down from just feeling his parent breathe this way.
- Get your child used to the word "no." Trying it on an airplane for the first time will only get you screams and resistance. Remember, setting clear boundaries and rules helps children to feel safe and cared for.
- Many children cry over the seat belt being put on. This can be practiced ahead of time by playing airplane at home prior to your trip or pretending the car is an airplane.
- Try to make sure your child has a good night's sleep prior to the trip. A well-rested child is your best defense.
- Massaging a child's hand, back, or feet can diffuse active energy.
- Remember to laugh. Laughter is a known stress reducer and can help many situations. Laugh at yourself when you might normally become angry. Teach your children to laugh at their own mistakes.

Parent's POV
On Air Travel with Kids

"Traveling with my two boys made me crazy. I was always one change of clothes shy. They ended up leaving the plane looking like they were in a food fight."—Sue

Know that you are not alone. Most parents feel helpless in the contained situation of an airplane. Even implementing time out is difficult on a plane. For children that need encouragement, a reward system for the flight can work wonders. You know your child best. Plan ahead so that you can have a stress-free trip!

—— Relax FAQ ——

Q: We're planning a cross-country road trip with our third- and fifth-graders this coming summer. How can we keep them engaged in the process? We want to create some amazing memories on this journey.

A: How wonderful! Before you head out on your long trip, sit down as a family with a map to discuss which cities might make good overnight stops. Everyone gets to pick an attraction that they'd like to visit along the route. That way, you all have something special to look forward to. You may need to help give ideas to your little ones, but they will surely enjoy being part of the planning process.

Hitting the Road

What if you're planning a road trip with the family and it's stressing you out? Here are a few favorite tips to make your road trip free and easy:

- **Routine and Sleep**—Make sure the children are well rested the night before. A well-rested child is a happier, calmer, well-balanced child.
- **Relax and Laugh**—Leave extra time for your trip. Make sure you have time to enjoy the journey. Stop for a picnic, or just stop to blow bubbles, or even fly a kite.
- **Be Creative and Entrust**—Make sure to give each of your kids their own camera or picture-taking device. It will motivate them to document their journey and encourage creativity.
- **Set Goals and Celebrate**—Set a time goal for good behavior in the car. And when you reach your goal, be sure to celebrate. Everyone's happy when you stop for an ice cream treat.

- **Be Prepared**—If you're traveling with younger children, be sure to pack a potty. It will save you lots of frantic moments.

MINDFUL MANTRA

Just for today, I realize that traveling and parenting is a journey.
Each day I can reset my sails and change my course.

CHAPTER 13

During the Holidays

"If you want to be happy, be."

—LEO TOLSTOY

⚬ LORI'S LESSON ⚭

Holidays are a magical time when children are full of hope, wishes, and dreams. It is my favorite time to incorporate relaxation techniques and jump onto a child's optimism train. It is impossible for stress, anxiety, or fear to exist when you are truly feeling the pure energy of hope. Holidays are a reminder to receive the gift of optimism and hope.

The holidays bring additional stress to everyone—adults and kids alike. But it is possible to raise your awareness during this time and monitor your family for signs of stress. Introducing relaxation strategies can keep everyone's mind, body, and spirit working in harmony during this joyful—but often harried—time.

> *Imagine . . .*
> Close your eyes, take a deep breath, and imagine what it would feel like to leave all of your expectations of family and holidays at the door. Step through the doorway into a room filled with love and hope.

MINDFUL MANTRA

Just for today, I will let go of expectations and step into happiness.

Because holidays are such a big part of our culture, it can be stressful for children when the pressure for holidays to be perfect becomes overbearing for the parents (remember, little ones absorb your stress!). It can also cause stress for children when holidays aren't acknowledged at home yet celebrated at school, the library, and other places they frequent. This means that celebrating holidays requires finding that sweet spot between retaining calm AND embracing the spirit of the season!

Here are ideas on how to minimize stress while creatively celebrating the major holidays:

VALENTINE'S DAY

Here are some ways to show those around you that you love them on Valentine's Day and every day:

- Play love-filled music all day long. Love songs by Frank Sinatra, Harry Connick Jr., or Steven Halpern's *Chakra Suite* help to fill the air with love and open your heart. Here is a link to get your playlist started: *http://amzn.to/16zjufD*.
- Shift from gifts to love. During dinner or breakfast, have each family member say one thing they love about the person sitting next to him or her.
- Be a little kinder, a little gentler, a little more tolerant, and a little more creative. Let kids decorate their rooms with hearts or strings of light.
- Keep it simple. Start the day with a candlelight breakfast. Use red or pink plates or put a plant or cactus with red blooms on the table.
- Watch your wedding video, or look through your wedding album as a family.
- Use loving affirmations such as, "I love myself" and "I am filled with love."
- Give extra, unexpected hugs and kisses to your children and spouse.
- Do a simple art activity that will have your kids loving themselves and their creativity. Drizzle or paint glue on a pre-cut heart. Let kids crunch up various colors of tissue paper. Stick anywhere and everywhere.
- Make a heart-shaped pizza (from scratch) with help from your children.
- Leave a special love note on your children and spouse's pillows. Put little notes on a mirror or other surprising places. (Little JOTS makes it easy. *http://littlejots.com/*)
- Incorporate your relaxation skills by visualizing your heart smiling, laughing, or even dancing.

ᴄᴇ LORI'S LESSON ᴈᴈ

As a young mom I welcomed the arrival of our first daughter two weeks before Valentine's Day. My husband was so blissfully in love with his new daughter, wife, and the celebration of a new life that he purchased Valentine's cards to honor every woman he knew: his mother; his sister; his baby daughter; my mother; my aunt; and even my neighbor! It sounds beautiful except for the simple fact that while he was in such a love-induced fog he forgot to acknowledge the very woman who spent many hours in labor only a few weeks prior—not one gushy, mushy card was for me.

My first reaction was to be hurt, offended, and angry, but then something took hold of me. I realized that Valentine's Day was a day to experience LOVE—not a test or an expectation of how someone else is supposed to express his love to you. Love is always nearby and available to anyone that wants to step into it. Love also begins with self. I loved myself for having been a catalyst for this joyful burst of love and random card giving.

ST. PATRICK'S DAY

You don't need to be Irish to tap into St. Patrick's Day. Put your own spin on this holiday to get your Irish (or not) eyes smiling and your soul relaxing. Playful family traditions reduce stress and strengthen relationships. Here are a few tips to eat, drink, and be merry and relaxed for St. Patrick's Day.

- Go Green: Brighten your day with green at your breakfast table. Use a green tablecloth. Put a green plant on the table: crocus, daffodil, or even a succulent will brighten the mood. Fun green plates or green candles can get your family in the mood for spring.
- Eat: Serve up an Irish dish or eat something green. Many kids will eat spinach dip, asparagus, or even edamame, especially when you tell them it is the food of leprechauns! No worries, if your kids don't eat corned beef and cabbage, you can find shamrock shaped ravioli at the market.

● Drink: Serve up a green vegetable drink. Try blending fresh kale, apple, and pineapple for a healthy, sweet treat or visit The Nutrition Mom and try her Green Butterfinger smoothie, found at *www.thenutritionmom.com/*.

● Be Merry: Wear green, listen to Irish music, and dance around the house. Do an Irish jig with the kids. Watch a few minutes of *River Dance* . . . and the kids will jump into action.

● Get Outside: Take the kids or whole family for a nature walk and look for signs of leprechauns. Use a camera and encourage children to take photos of clues. Have a green item scavenger hunt. See how many green things you can find and make a list.

● Create: Storytelling or story creating is a fun way to foster creativity, laughter, and relaxation. Sit outside or around the dinner table and create a progressive story. Each family member can add a portion of the story—A leprechaun woke up under a mushroom with one of his pointy shoes missing—Create a story where everything is green!

● Arts and Crafts: Use lots of gold and green to make a leprechaun house out of an old shoebox or cereal box. Finger paint with shades of green. Look for clover and press them into the paint. Go green and use items from your recycling bin.

● Relax: The color green can be used to rejuvenate, calm, or heal. Sit quietly and visualize the color green filling every cell in your body. Focus on breathing in healing green air and out healing green air. See the green filling your lungs and heart. (*A Boy and a Turtle* and *Bubble Riding* found on *Indigo Ocean Dreams,* are both visualization stories that teach children to relax with colors.)

STRESS-LESS ACTIVITY: KEEP THE MAGIC ALIVE

Have each child leave a shoe outside their door with something shiny in it to entice a leprechaun to leave a piece of candy, flower, shamrock, note, or little gift. If you can leave the shoes outside, use green sidewalk chalk to make shamrocks or arrows to lead the leprechauns to your shoe. For indoors make a path with cutouts from construction paper. With a little luck, a leprechaun will visit while the little ones sleep and leave a surprise.

EASTER

Holidays are a wonderful excuse to reconnect with family, share stories, look for signs of hope, explore relaxation, and spark your creativity. It doesn't matter if you celebrate a particular holiday, or you just want to believe that a giant bunny hops from house to house hiding eggs. Use this hopeful holiday to create your own family day:

- Put some carrots in the mailbox for the Easter Bunny or to invite spring to visit. When the kids are sleeping, be sure to sneak out and leave a few nibble marks.
- Hide plastic eggs with words in them. When the kids collect all of the words they can work together to assemble them into a sentence. The sentence is a clue to where their present is hidden. For more than one child, use a different color of paper for each child's sentence.
- Think outside of the candy box. A gift can be tickets to a movie, clothes, jump ropes, seeds, or toys. *(One year my children were surprised to receive bags of wildflower seeds with instructions to disperse them on a nearby hill.)*
- Encourage emotional intelligence and stress management. Print out positive statements or affirmations and glue them onto eggs. "I am starting fresh." "I am growing." "I am full of life." Experience and talk about rabbit energy. Hop around like a rabbit and float on a breeze like a bird. Discuss when it is good to use rabbit energy and when it is helpful to have bird energy. Talk about the colors of the eggs and flowers. Do the different colors evoke different feelings? Does light blue make you feel

relaxed? Does orange make you feel happy? How does holding the egg make you feel? Is it relaxing to roll it around in your hands? Can you look at an egg and only think of the egg for any amount of time? How does it feel to stop the chatter in your head?

- Share and learn what eggs symbolize to various cultures. Discuss your religious symbolism or create your own personal meaning. Encourage children to share what an egg means to them. Is it a celebration of new life, rebirth, new chances, new hope? Does it represent the circle of life, abundance, newness, feeling strong, feeling fragile, breaking out of a shell?

HALLOWEEN

Here are some of my top Halloween tips to avoid meltdowns!

- Be flexible. Do not allow your definitions of a fun Halloween define your child's expectation of fun. It is not necessary for children to have the full-blown experience in order for them to have a good time. If your child wants to answer the door and hand out candy, then let him do that without guilt. If your child wants to sit on the porch and costume watch, then let him. If he just wants to go to bed, tuck him into bed . . . Trust me, it will not matter when they go to college!

- Decide and let children know ahead of time how many pieces of candy they are allowed to eat while trick-or-treating and after. Have them keep the wrappers to keep count. When they ask for more . . . ask them to count how many wrappers they have and let them answer their own question.

- Head home before your child becomes tired. Do not wait for the meltdown. It helps to let your child know ahead of time how long she will have to trick-or-treat.

- Consider your child's needs. If she does not do well in a noisy group, schedule a friend for her to trick-or-treat with and stay away from the crowds.
- Costumes! Most kids do not want to put a jacket over their costume. Direct your child to a weather-appropriate costume and consider having them wear long johns under the costume. The younger your child is the bigger the comfort issue becomes. If your child has sensory issues, costume comfort is a priority. Bring comfortable shoes if your child refuses to leave the glass Cinderella slippers at home. Colored sweatpants and a sweatshirt with a hood make an easy costume. Bright yellow with a pair of sunglasses and you have a sun. Sew strips of fabric, yarn, or ears on a hood and you have a lion or a rainbow. Don't fret if you can't sew. Safety pins or hem binding tape are options.
- Eat dinner before leaving the house. Remember that a nutritionally balanced child is better able to handle stressors.
- Go early with young children—before it gets dark.
- Too much candy for one family? No problem. Let your child select a handful of candy and leave the rest at the foot of the bed for the Halloween Fairy! If the fairy likes the candy, she will take it and leave a surprise gift or a thank you note sprinkled with fairy dust in its place.
- If your child has dietary restrictions, no problem. Let her collect the candy and sell it to you afterwards. Items with peanuts get 5 cents each. Assign different values for different types. Kids love this exercise and will spend hours sorting the candy into their value groups. Take your child to her favorite store and let her spend her candy money on a treat she can eat!

THANKSGIVING

How can anyone resist a holiday that rallies around family and giving thanks?

G-R-A-T-E-F-U-L Thanksgiving Tips

G – Gratitude is the opposite of stress. It is difficult to feel stressed-out when we are feeling gratitude.

R – Relax your expectations and let the day unfold. You might be surprised by the outcome.

A – Acceptance is the opposite of judgment. If we accept our family members for who they are and what they are capable of, we can relax and enjoy ourselves.

T – Tweens can be a helpful part of Thanksgiving. Ask them what they would like to *bring to the table*. Let them bring it.

E – Engage children and let them help with age-appropriate assignments, for example, putting the nuts out or making the centerpiece. Let them do it their way . . . not your way.

F – Focus on family for this day. Put all work and worries on the shelf.

U – Unplug the electronics for dinner so that everyone can be fully present.

L – Love is often overlooked when we are busy. Cook with love . . . Speak with love . . . Show your love and gratitude for your family on this Thanksgiving Day.

Parent's POV
On Gratitude at the Holidays

"It feels like the most important things can be easily overlooked in the hustle of getting everything ready for the holidays. I will have a full house this Thanksgiving—which can be stressful—but I am going to make a point of cooking and speaking with love and showing gratitude!" —Anna

CHRISTMAS AND CHANUKAH

Which vision describes holiday time at your house? Visions of sugarplums dancing in your head? Or visions of shopping, late nights, no school, no schedule, candy, apple pie, parties, company, and travel? If you picked the latter, then you are in the company of most families!

Christmas, Chanukah, Kwanzaa, Winter Solstice . . . whichever holiday you celebrate you can do it with *stress-free style*. What better time to integrate stress management and relaxation into your family's holiday celebration and life? Here are some tips to get you there:

- Be aware that constant company and holiday social interaction is exhausting and stressful for you *and* your children. If you are spending extended time visiting your relatives or vice versa, allow for breaks from your relatives. Take your kids out to the park, a movie, or even a candy-store run without the entire entourage of cousins, aunts, and uncles. Your sleepover company will also appreciate the break.
- Avoid parties that overwhelm your children. Try having smaller, more intimate gatherings instead of one big blowout. Pay attention to your children's eating schedule. You may need to prepare them a small meal or healthy snack to hold them over on party days.
- Familiarize your children with unfamiliar relatives prior to the holiday. Look at photos of Aunt Mary and Uncle Jim so your children are more comfortable when they meet them at a party or social gathering. Play a fun memory game with the photos, associating names with faces!
- Give your children age-appropriate assignments to help make the holiday joyful and memorable. Involving your children creates memories, increases self-esteem, and strengthens family bonds. Your children are capable of filling a cheese platter, making place cards, setting the table, and many other simple tasks. (Resist the urge to redo their contribution . . . let the napkin remain on the wrong side of the plate.)

● Keep various Christmas hats, dreidels, gameday pom poms, maracas, jingle bells, Mardi Gras necklaces, antlers, elf shoes, streamers, batons, flags, tambourines, crazy socks, animal eye masks, and a few old pots and pans with wooden spoons for banging in an open, nearby container—it's creative fun for kids, teens, and adults! Join in and lead a parade around your apartment or house. Laugh and you will enjoy less stress and more joy. Film it and share with your relatives during the holidays. Youngsters want your time more than presents. *(Do I hear spontaneous music and laughing?)* View our family holiday video and more on our *Stress Free Kids* YouTube channel *http://youtu.be/8TJ25uyapbQ*.

MINDFUL MANTRA
*Just for today, I will keep my heart open
and ready to accept new experiences.*

Stress negatively impacts the moods of others, but happiness spreads like wildfire! You have the ability to spread happiness, especially during the holidays. The American Psychological Association noted that 91 percent of children are aware of their parents' stress. Holidays bring an increase in emotions, spending, entertaining, traveling, changes in routine, and family stress. By following these tips you automatically make room for more joy.

SANITY SAVER   Try to do your adult shopping sans children! Avoid taking your children when you need to make frequent stops to various stores. Continually getting in and out of the car can grate on everyone's nerves. Do take your children shopping when you are going to a kid-friendly store and can incorporate their help in finding a gift for a specific person. Keep the actual amount of time spent on shopping age appropriate.

—— Relax FAQ ——

Q: How can I create a stress-free holiday that supports the needs of my special needs child?

A: Holiday crowds, lights, noise, strangers, hugging, change in routine, and chaos. This is a recipe for stress and sensory overload during the holidays for many children. As a parent you need to be flexible with your own definition of what a holiday should look like—your childhood traditions and rituals just may not work with your special needs child. Try to create new memories and redefine what holidays look like for your own family.

Set up a safe break space: Your child can enjoy downtime when they feel overstimulated at your house or at your relatives' houses. Set up a brain break space and be sure that the other children and guests know that this space is off-limits. Empower your special needs child to recognize when they need to go to their brain break space. Practice ahead of time helping your child to recognize when his mood is escalating. Children can pack a relaxation bag they can go to if they are feeling anxious. Bring earphones and their special relaxation music or stories. Play-Doh, a stress ball, music, a video game, even a camera can help children relax and give them a focus if they have social anxiety.

Get ready: Social stories, books, and movies can be a big help in preparing your child emotionally for holidays. Comfortable clothing and small-dose exposures to holiday sounds can help physically. Think ahead with an eye for anxiety causing issues. Is wrapping paper too loud? Use easy open bags or just decorate with a bow. Are the electronic bears with bells at Grandma's house going to cause sensory overload? Ask her to unplug them before you get there. Let friends and family know about triggers ahead of time. If your child doesn't like to be hugged suggest a handshake or just a wave. Your friends, family, and special needs children will be glad you did.

STRESS-LESS ACTIVITY: HOLIDAY DINING

Slow down the hectic holiday pace by changing the way you eat dinner. Move your table closer to the Christmas tree or set up a picnic blanket near the Menorah. Shut the ceiling lights off and eat by the lights of the tree, candles, or flashlights—so peaceful and something different for the kids.

NEW YEAR'S EVE

When you have kids New Year's Eve takes on a whole new meaning. Here are some ways you can incorporate your children into the celebration—while still enjoying an "adult" evening, too!

- Schedule age-appropriate celebrations for your children. If they are young think about turning the clock back by two or three hours. Celebrate New Year's at 9:00 P.M. with your kids, put them to bed, then continue your party with the adults to ring in the New Year at midnight.
- Replace making a New Year's resolution with a New Year's reflection! Have each family member speak about one or two accomplishments or goals they have reached this past year. For example, your 5-year-old may have just learned to read, or your tween may have made first chair in the band. Focus on the positive from the past instead of making promises to stop something in the future.
- Instead of using champagne as your symbol for celebration, how about toasting with sparkling cider? This is the time for everyone to mention their hopes for the new year.
- Too tired to stay up late? Move your celebration to New Year's Day. Start a new tradition by gathering for a special festive New Year's Day breakfast or brunch.
- Make some noise by banging pots and pans, or for a softer celebration, blow bubbles to bring in the new year. Visualize blowing

away any stress or resentments from the past year. Ask your children what hopes they would like to put into their bubbles for the new year.

STRESS-LESS ACTIVITY: COLD WEATHER BREATHING

For added winter fun, practice your new deep breathing techniques when it is cold outside. Kids get the added visual of seeing their exhalations turn into vapor.

CHAPTER 14

When a Loved One Passes Away

"Breathe. Let go. And remind yourself that this very moment is the only one you know you have for sure."

—OPRAH WINFREY

℮ℓ LORI'S LESSON ℘℧

When I was a young teenager, I tried to wake my grandmother from her daily pre-dinner nap when I realized that my grandmother was dead. The adults around me began to scream and I was pushed aside. I felt scared and alone. My mom did not know how to cope with her own sadness and pain. Her grief turned into depression and my own feelings were not acknowledged or addressed. It is important to realize that children and teens are not equipped with the skills needed to cope with the loss of a loved one. Parents dealing with their own grief may not recognize that their children are also stepping into an unknown territory of raw emotions never experienced before. Grief is one of the most misunderstood emotions we can experience. Parents can lead the way to healing.

Imagine . . .
Close your eyes, take a deep breath, and imagine that you are hugging your departed loved one or pet. Repeat: "I miss you, I love you, thank you for being part of my world."

My colleague, Wendy Young, LMSW, BCD, is a mom of three, an award-winning child and adolescent therapist, and the founder of Kidlutions: Solutions for Kids (*www.kidlutions.com*). She is the author of *How Long Does the Sad Last?: A Workbook for Grieving Children*. She has helped thousands of children worldwide cope with grief and has developed grief programming for fourteen school districts. Here, she shows you how to help your child cope with the death of a loved one.

Helping Grieving Children

It's hard to put the words "children" and "grieving" into the same sentence, as it's natural to think of the childhood years as carefree and wondrous. However, children also suffer loss, and when they do, they look to the adults in their lives to help them through.

No matter how prepared you are to raise healthy, happy kids, you may not be equipped to help them deal with grief—and you're not alone. It's not something adults like to think about, nor is it something adults envision having to do. However, when the unthinkable happens, you need to know how you can best help support your kids as they go through the grieving process.

MINDFUL MANTRA

Just for today, I will be completely honest about how I am feeling. I will encourage my children to share how they feel. Emotional honesty is a gift.

Explaining Death to Children: All Living Things Die

It is often helpful to explain death to your child by first explaining life. When people are alive they breathe, see, hear, smell, taste, and feel. You can feel their heart beat and see their chest rise and fall as they take a breath. Their body is working and they are alive. When someone is dead, they do not breathe, see, hear, smell, taste, or feel. They cannot hear you or answer you. Their body has stopped working and they are dead.

All living things die: flowers, trees, pets, and people. Anything that lives will someday die. Most people live a very, very, very long time. When you see dead bugs, birds, or other animals (even leaves and flowers), use them as teachable moments.

Calling It What It Is

Use the words *death*, *dying*, *dead*. This may seem harsh, but it is very necessary to help kids delineate that death is a very different state than any other. Avoid euphemisms: Saying any of the following to children, "She's sleeping" (this may induce sleep difficulties and fears); "He went on a long trip" (this may prompt the question, when is he coming back?); "We 'lost' grandpa" (this may beg the question, when will we find him again?); and "Grandma's gone away for a while" only add to the confusion surrounding a death.

Terminal Illness

Explain to your child that doctors can almost always help us feel better (sore throats, headaches, stomachaches, illnesses), but sometimes a body is so sick that the doctors cannot help. In those cases, the doctors have good medicine to help our loved one be comfortable and out of pain, but there are times when they cannot keep our loved person alive. Doctors always try their best to keep people alive—but sometimes it's just not possible.

Parent's POV
On Understanding Death

"My 5-year-old daughter sat both of her grandmas down for a serious talk. She told them that some grandmas die and some grandmas don't. Her matter-of-fact delivery surprised all of us. She reassured them both that she herself was going to live a long, long time. I was astonished at her openness and willingness to talk about death." —Peter

Prepare Them

If your child is going to attend a wake or funeral for the first time, you'll want to thoroughly prepare him for what he will see, hear, and experience. Explain what a casket is, that the deceased will no longer be able to talk, breathe, eat, or feel pain. Explain to your child that there may be many emotions and tears and that it's okay when people cry because they are sad. They just miss their loved one. Let your child know that it's okay for him to cry because crying gets the sad out.

SANITY SAVER   Coping with the death of someone you loved obviously takes a large emotional toll on you and your family. Make sure you are getting enough rest and proper nutrition during this time so that you can properly handle the pressures you face. If you don't feel up to even simple self-care, enlist a close friend who is not grieving (perhaps she didn't know the person who passed) to help you stay on track in these basic areas.

When Your Pet Passes Away: Meaningful Ways to Support Your Child

Always tell the truth. When given the truth in an age-appropriate manner, children can cope. The truth is always preferable to saying something like, "Fluffy ran away." Your child will eventually learn the truth and dishonesty can erode your child's trust in you. While it might seem like a kind-hearted thing to do, trying to soften the blow of the death does not help your child. He cannot forever be shielded from the reality of death, and helping him learn to cope with loss is far more important than trying to shield him from the feelings of grief. It provides a much healthier approach.

Avoid euphemisms. When discussing the death of the loved animal, do not say, "Sam is sleeping, he is peaceful." This may induce a fear of bedtime in young children. Avoid saying, "We lost Princess." This implies you may find her again.

Be patient. Young children may need to continue to talk about their pet's death in order to understand it. They may also play the death out with stuffed animals or toys. Do not suggest your child "find something else to do," or play something "nice." It's important *not* to view this kind of play as "macabre." This is how **≫**

children make sense of the loss, especially in the early days. Use their play content as a springboard for more discussion. Be sure to use "feeling" words. "Your stuffed animal died, just like Sparky. It is SAD when our animals die. I know you miss Sparky very much. I do, too."

Support your child in memorializing your pet. Whether or not you have your beloved pet's body for burial, you can find a way to engage your child in a ritual to memorialize the animal. You can find a special area in your yard to perhaps plant a small bush or some flowers and make a marker with you pet's name. Another option would be to have a small resin or plaster garden creature that symbolizes your beloved pet. If you live in an apartment, a small potted plant or just a framed picture of the animal could be used. Allow each family member to say something special about the pet, something they will miss, and something funny or silly that they remember about the pet.

Share your own grief. Let your child see you grieve. It is helpful for a child to know that you, too, loved and miss the pet. Express to your child that you feel great sadness, but that you also hold many dear memories of the pet. Talk with your child often about the pet.

Hug your child. Always hug your children, but even more so when they have experienced a loss. Children need more TLC when they are grieving. If your child doesn't want to talk about the pet, encourage him to either write or draw about it.

ᏌᏣ LORI'S LESSON ᏣᏓ

A few weeks after our beloved pet died, the vet surprised us by sending us our dog's paw print along with a donation made in our pet's name to the local animal hospital. This simple act facilitated healing for my entire family. Ask your vet if they provide this service, or involve your family by donating time or cash to your local pet shelter or hospital.

STRESS-LESS ACTIVITY: CREATE A MEMORY BOX

Use an old shoebox or other suitable container and have your child decorate the "Memory Box." Have your child and family members select things that remind them of your pet. Perhaps it's a collar, a toy that belonged to your pet, or pictures of happy times with your pet. Family members can even write little notes or snippets of memories about your pet. When your child or other family members are feeling particularly sad, they can sift through the "Memory Box," and find evidence of happy times spent inside.

CHAPTER 15

When Terror Strikes

*"When I was a boy and I would see
scary things in the news, my mother would
say to me, 'Look for the helpers. You will
always find people who are helping.'"*
—FRED ROGERS

ᴄᴇ LORI'S LESSON ᴐᴏ

"A tomato is coming, a tomato is coming." These are the words my neighbor's son was yelling as the group of kids hunkered down in the basement while the tornado sirens were blaring. My daughter was terrified and I realized that it is not the actual word (tornado, tsunami, shooting, or bomb) that terrifies children; it is the emotion behind the words. It is the way in which we deliver information. Fear and anxiety can be delivered or transferred to a child with even the safest nonthreatening words—doesn't matter if it is tomato or tornado.

Between floods, tornados, hurricanes, plane crashes, bombings, and school shootings, there are a lot of events that are beyond your control that can cause deep stress for your children if they aren't properly addressed at home. In this chapter, you'll learn coping mechanisms that are age appropriate to help your little ones begin to process and understand how to handle stress in times of tragedy and devastation.

When Terror Hits Close to Home

The Boston Marathon bombing sent a wave of shock, fear, and stress through families across the world. Children are vulnerable when faced with these types of tragedies and do not have experience coping with these extreme feelings and concerns. As parents, you'd love to believe we live in a safe world and that we do all that we can to protect our children. After witnessing how in a quick instant everything can change and safe places no longer seem safe, it's natural to begin to wonder how you can protect your family. When you question your own safety, your fears can trickle down and add to the uncertainty your children are feeling. When tragedy strikes, such as in the case of the recent Boston Marathon bombing, your children were likely exposed to the graphic content. Children and adults ask fear-filled questions: What happens next? Am I safe? Where might the next attack be? Who did this? So how can you help your children understand these events and reduce any anxiety they may be experiencing? Here are several tips to keep your child's stress to a minimum:

- **Limit exposure to media coverage.** This is important for reducing stress in children. A constant reminder of how their world has been torn apart builds overwhelming anxiety and fear. Monitor what they are watching on television, and online. Encourage conversation about what they have seen and heard. (Keep in mind that young children might think that the event is happening over and over again—they may not realize they are witnessing the same scene.)
- **Listen and acknowledge.** Honor your child's feelings of fear, sadness, or worry. Provide comfort with hugs and positive words designed to help your child feel safe. Find out what your children have heard from other sources including their friends. Children often share misinformation with each other. Imaginations can also take over and stories become inaccurate and embellished.
- **Make sure it's age appropriate.** It takes extra special vigilance to provide age-appropriate information. A 5-year-old should not be hearing or seeing the same details that a 15-year-old would be exposed to. Be careful not to share your adult fears with your children. A child is not your therapist, friend, or emotional dumping ground.
- **Restore routine.** Getting your kids back into their routine as soon as possible restores a feeling of predictability and safety. Try to maintain family mealtime to provide familiarity, and an extra place for family-time communication.
- **Focus on good people and look for the helpers.** Mr. Rogers offers good advice. Somewhere deep inside each one of us human beings is a longing to know that all will be well. Our children need to hear from us adults that we will do everything

we can to keep them safe and to help them grow in this world. Children needed to be reminded that most people are good.

- **Pay extra attention to bedtime routine.** No matter what is going on in the world, children deserve to fall asleep peacefully. Read a happy story, listen to a relaxation CD, or explore soothing music. (*Indigo Dreams* CD series offers stories with relaxation techniques and music designed for children.)
- **Set a healthy example.** Studies show that a child's worries can be reduced if he learns habits that help him reduce anxieties—such as sharing worries, normalizing expectations, practicing relaxation, and others—that he can use the rest of his life. It's up to you to teach your kids coping strategies so they can use them to help them deal with whatever troubling event they encounter. Provide reassuring support. Our kids copy how we cope with our fears. So be the example of how to handle your own worries that you want your child to copy. Keep your worries or pessimism in check especially during a tragedy or after a trauma.

SANITY SAVER   During times of crisis, unplug the TV. Otherwise, you can get sucked into an unhealthy barrage of tragic images and commentary that doesn't help you or your little ones move forward in healing.

My colleague, Jodi S. DiNatale, PsyD, is a certified school psychologist and licensed educational psychologist who has been practicing for twenty years. As part of the School Threat Assessment and Response Team, she visits schools that have experienced a traumatic event to assist in the development and implementation of crisis plans that support the staff, students, and community. Here, she shares her tips for how to help your child cope in times of crisis.

The Path to Recovery

On your journey through life, you go through different stages and reach certain milestones within particular timeframes. Along this journey, different events happen that can change your worldview, as well as how you engage in your everyday life. When terror strikes, whether it's a natural disaster (e.g., a super storm, hurricane, tornado, flash flooding, etc.), or an act of violence (e.g., 9/11, Sandy Hook Elementary School shooting, Boston Marathon bombing, etc.), fear, anxiety, worry, and sadness often become a part of our lives in an instant. Depending on the degree of your involvement— whether you are directly involved in such an event or you hear about it on the news—these tragedies shift our attention, remind us that scary things can happen, and put many people in a state of shock. After working through the disbelief of the situation, people often begin to look for ways to pick up the pieces and move forward. As parents, you may feel uneasy about what to say to your children, how to answer their questions, how to get things back on track, and return to your "normal" lives. Following the guidelines outlined here and being aware of certain issues can help to bring peace back into your lives.

Remember that the effects of these events can be longstanding for some children, especially those directly involved. The time it takes to process such events can vary from person to person, and the anniversary of an incident can also have an impact on people. Being aware of these factors when coping with a traumatic event will help you get through it more effectively. Doing activities that help you cope with the feelings and issues related to the events are important in the healing process. Remember to take the time to listen to your children and give them extra support and attention, be it by playing a game with them, reading, or having some special time together. It all goes a long way in helping everyone to cope.

MINDFUL MANTRA
*Just for today, I will remind myself that this is
an unusual circumstance, and that in this moment,
I am safe and my child is safe.*

Pay attention to changes in your child's behavior, eating habits, sleeping routine, and reactions to stress and small challenges. During such experiences, people's frustration tolerance is often lower causing them to have more significant reactions to minor issues. While this may occur initially, further support should be sought if these issues continue after approximately two weeks.

Watch for "triggers," which are things that set your child off and remind him of the event. These triggers can include words, sounds, and images that seem to cue him to think about or experience the feelings of the incident. This can often occur in children with special needs and it is important to communicate these triggers to the people who work with your child.

Explain the range of emotions your children might feel due to the events they have experienced and that it is okay to have these feelings. These emotions may include shock/disbelief, fear, guilt, grief, confusion, shame/loss, and anger. The degree and range of these emotions depend on the level of involvement and developmental age of your child. Remember that knowledge is power and if your child knows what to expect, it is easier for him to cope with the issue.

Use your resources. Be open to using resources in your community and be sure to consult with your child's school so that you know what is being told to your child regarding the incident. Make teachers and counselors aware of issues your child is having so they can provide support as appropriate. The National Association of School Psychologists has an excellent website (*www.nasponline.org*) that provides parents and educators with tips on how to handle such events.

Parent's POV
On National Events That Are Shocking

"During this time kids need to feel safe, calm, and reassured every step of the way. The best thing we can do during these times is to bring peace and calm to ourselves and no matter what changes need to be made externally the kids will feel at ease if the parents are. Be open and honest about the changes in the world (age appropriate, of course) and gather as a team, even ask their suggestions for changes." —Melinda

Imagine . . .
Close your eyes, take a deep breath, and imagine that you and your family are surrounded by peaceful situations and loving people.

Children and Natural Disasters: How to Help Them Cope

It's no secret that natural disasters have a way of uprooting lives and tearing communities apart. Hurricane Sandy has devastated the lives of thousands in the Northeast, most of whom are still working tirelessly to get their lives back to normal. Children, in particular, thrive in a structured environment, which becomes nonexistent in times of a natural disaster. Families are still struggling with obtaining basic life necessities, while trying to stay mentally sound. Dealing with the aftermath of Hurricane Sandy has left families and entire communities with questions of how to find peace and structure among the chaos and confusion. Here are a few things you can do to help reduce stress and anxiety for your children during these uncertain times:

Reestablishing a routine is beneficial to children and the family as a whole. While this may be difficult if you have lost your home or if you are still without power, establishing a routine will help your family cope with the many changes in their everyday life. Sharing meals together and allotting chores are just few ways to make children feel as though they are in a stable environment and therefore less stressed.

Creating activities for children will draw their attention away from the disaster and have them focus on a more positive task. If without power, turn towards activities such as coloring or drawing to help your child lower their anxiety levels and enjoy the familiarity of creativity.

Keeping communication open will help your family stay connected by expressing shared thoughts and fears. Parents should make sure they create a comfortable environment for their children to express their worries or concerns.

Ongoing and reassuring communication is a key element in reducing stress levels. If children are withdrawn and unwilling to talk, they may feel more comfortable expressing their feelings through drawings, journal entries, or stories. Art, music, and drama can be a healthy means of communication and should be promoted. Do not burden your children with your adult-level fears and concerns. Instead, address and support your child's fears so that you can add your hope and optimism. Times of tragedy can take an emotional toll on children, so make sure to lend an ear and work towards an understanding together. Children are looking to you for safety, stability, and leadership.

Limiting exposure to media coverage is important for reducing stress in children. A constant reminder of how their world has been torn apart builds overwhelming anxiety and distress. Monitor what they are watching and encourage conversation about what they have seen.

Connecting with other disaster victims can help parents and children immensely. Understanding that others have suffered can help you cope with your own experience. Sharing "next-step" ideas with one another can also help to work towards a new future, and perhaps introduce positive ways to move forward that you may not have realized. Socializing also steers the mind away from focusing on the negatives in the past.

Sharing your plan with your children of how your family is going to stay safe and begin a new life with a positive outcome is important in moving forward. Often adults assume that children understand what's happening, but children have very vivid imaginations and tend to project the most negative outcomes.

Keeping your children safe during the aftermath of a natural disaster is imperative. Especially if you are currently residing in a shelter, use masking tape on the inside of your children's clothing or a piece of paper in their pocket with their name, age, parents' names, and cell phone numbers. This is especially important for children with special needs.

Listening to relaxing music and stories is a great way to salvage peace of mind through these troubling times. Relaxation stories can help your children feel peaceful, and even help them sleep better in an unfamiliar place. You can download *Indigo Ocean Dreams* to your iTunes library.

LORI'S LESSON

Tornado warnings, severe thunderstorms, and taking cover in the basement occur frequently in my city. To reduce fear and chaos when the alarms go off, we helped our daughter create, prepare, and decorate her own safe spot. She has a warm blanket, stuffed animal, pen and writing pad, flashlight attached to the wall with a string, and nail polish. By including her in developing a safe refuge, we helped her to feel less vulnerable during frightening weather.

STRESS-LESS ACTIVITY: MAKE PRAYER OR "WISH" FLAGS

Facilitate healing by creating flags (based on Tibetan prayer flags) with your family. Encourage children to write a prayer, a healing thought, a good wish, or just draw a smiley face. Hang them outside or near a window with the thought that the wind will carry the message to the survivors, victims, and children affected by the tragedy.

How to Make Prayer Flags:

1. Cut pieces of fabric or lightweight paper to 5" × 11". (Use materials you already have at home, or go to a crafts store and check out the remnant fabric bin.)
2. Fold the top down on each piece of fabric or paper and stitch or glue it in place to create a 3" sleeve, making the flag surface 5" × 8".
3. Decorate the flags using paint, magic marker, stickers, or if your kids are really crafty, by embroidering them—add words, pictures, and symbols as desired. However you choose to decorate the flags, they are meant to represent your feelings of hope, comfort, and love that you want to send out into the world.
4. Thread the flags onto a string or cord and hang them outdoors so the breeze will catch them and spread your good intentions! You can also hang them inside near a window (or anyplace that will remind your children of the sentiment behind them).

(For inspiration, check out images of flags from The Prayer Flag Project on Flickr: www.flickr.com/groups/1715420@N23/.)

CONCLUSION

Staying Stress Free as a Family

"Trust yourself. You know more than you think you do."

—DR. BENJAMIN SPOCK

During many of my parenting days, I felt like I was navigating uncharted waters without a life jacket. I remember when the hospital "let" me take my baby home. I thought to myself, "Really? Are they kidding me?" Parenting is an ever-evolving journey that presents new and unexpected challenges at every turn. I may not always have the answers, but I do know I can control how I respond and that I can access the tools I need to find a place of calm within myself. I do know that when I make mistakes, I can acknowledge them, apologize, and show my children that I can make the decision to do the next right thing.

You know this already: A parent's job is one of the most rewarding—and most difficult. While you love your children dearly, the pressures you feel to raise them "right"—instilling them with your values while keeping them safe and buffered from the worries of the adult world—can feel overwhelming some days.

By reading this book you are at a turning point. You have stepped into joy-based parenting and you are equipped with the tools you need to transform your family. You can now enhance your parenting experience by integrating practical stress-reducing solutions into your daily living. More than anything, you should take away the idea that parenting really takes a village—you are not alone in this! To help keep your family feeling stress free as a way of life, be sure to reach out and share your experiences, hopes, and dreams with other parents, either via real-time meet-ups in your town or online. (Social media is a tremendous outlet to meet like-minded parents and support each other—find @StressFreeKids on Twitter, Facebook, and Pinterest for daily inspirational parenting tips.) When you work together, parents can find and share solutions that work for their children.

Stay persistent—and rely on your intuition and creativity. It is worth it when you see your child manage a moment in a calmer manner than the day before. Take time to breathe and celebrate the

small accomplishments. You and your children are now active participants in creating your own collection of stress-free moments. Smile,
take a deep breath, and know that the rewards of peaceful parenting
are . . . peaceful parenting.

STRESS FREE KIDS®
RESOURCES

All books, CDs, and curriculum are available in digital and app formats at *www.StressFreeKids.com.*

CDs and downloads:

Indigo Dreams
Four relaxation bedtime stories incorporate breathing, visualizations, muscular relaxation, and affirmations. Children follow along with the characters as they learn belly breathing with *A Boy and a Bear*, make positive statements with *The Affirmation Web*, visualize with *A Boy and a Turtle*, and relax with *The Goodnight Caterpillar*. Shorter stories are perfect for shorter attention spans and beginners ages 4–9. An additional music track and sounds of nature further enhance the experience.

Indigo Ocean Dreams
Four relaxation and stress-management stories for children help improve sleep, manage stress, and lower anxiety and anger. Children follow along with their sea friends as they learn to release and manage anger with *Angry Octopus*, build self-esteem with *Affirmation Weaver*, implement breathing with *Sea Otter Cove*, and visualize with *Bubble Riding*. Longer stories are ideal for older children ages 6–12. An additional music track and sounds of nature further enhance the experience.

Indigo Dreams: Garden of Wellness

Five children's stories designed to reduce worry, stress, and anger, while increasing healthy body image and self-esteem. Children follow along with the characters as they use positive statements to build self-esteem and make healthy food choices with *Caterpillar Choices*. *The Perfect Club* encourages self-acceptance and tolerance of others. Children learn emotional coping techniques of breathing and visualizing to release angry, hurt, or sad feelings that might arise from being excluded or teased. These children's stories are ideal for kids ages 5–11.

Indigo Dreams: Adult Relaxation

Experience four straightforward, no-nonsense relaxation techniques that help you to be a relaxed parent and achieve a deep state of sleep. Learn four stress-management techniques: breathing, affirmations, visualizations, and muscular relaxation accompanied by soothing, uplifting music to further enhance your relaxation experience. Written for moms and dads.

Indigo Teen Dreams: 2-CD Set

Now teens can explore the same relaxation and self-esteem-building techniques as the rest of the family. Guided instructional format introduces breathing, visualizing, muscle relaxation, and affirmations. Give teens the tools they need to reduce stress and anger. An additional full hour of relaxation music helps teens achieve a deeper state of sleep.

Music:

Indigo Dreams: Kid's Relaxation Music

Children drift off to sleep while enjoying dolphins, laughing with fireflies, exploring the rainforest, and walking on the moon. Kids love relaxing with *Dolphin Dance, Firefly Flight, Rain Forest,* and *Red*

Moon. Each track is masterfully created to entertain children while evoking a relaxation response. Child-friendly melodies and sounds of nature help children achieve a deep state of relaxation and sleep.

Indigo Dreams: Kid's Rainforest Relaxation Music

Worry, fear, and anxiety melt away as each track draws you deep into the rainforest with healing melodies and sounds of nature designed to delight your senses while creating a state of restful relaxation. Your whole family will love relaxing with *Forest Fantasy*, *Owl Song*, *Dream Keeper*, and *Amazon Whisper*. This enchanting hour of music will enhance sleep, decrease stress, and encourage creative thinking.

Stress Free Kids® Curriculum

This turnkey stress-management curriculum includes six books and two CDs (*Indigo Dreams* and *Indigo Ocean Dreams*). Stress Free Kids® stories, lesson plans, songs, movement, music, and worksheets introduce the four research-based techniques of positive statements, progressive muscle relaxation, visualizing, and breathing. This fun and interactive format makes stress management teachable for parents, youth leaders, guidance counselors, teachers, therapists, yoga instructors, and homeschoolers. Each lesson is designed to introduce practical solutions to daily living.

Books, eBooks, Apps

From the *Indigo Ocean Dreams Collection*:

Angry Octopus

This anger-management story introduces active progressive muscular relaxation and deep breathing. Children learn to unwind, relax, and control anger with this fun exercise known as progressive muscular relaxation. This engaging story quiets the mind and relaxes the body so your child can let go of anger, relax, and fall asleep peacefully.

Sea Otter Cove

Children love to experience belly breathing with playful sea otters and a sea child. This effective, self-calming technique, also known as diaphragmatic breathing, can have a positive impact on your child's health. Proper breathing can lower stress and anxiety levels. Delightful characters in this story and easy breathing encourage your child to slow down, relax, and fall asleep peacefully.

Affirmation Weaver

This believe-in-yourself story is designed to help children increase self-esteem with the use of positive statements. This technique can be used to manage stress, increase optimism, and accomplish goals. This encouraging story will bring a smile to your face and give your child a tool that will last a lifetime.

Bubble Riding

Children learn a fun visualization technique as they go on a bubble ride where they experience filling and relaxing their bodies with the colors of the rainbow. The colorful imagery in this story quiets the mind and relaxes the body so your child can manage stress, fall asleep peacefully, and so much more.

From the *Indigo Dreams Collection*:

The Goodnight Caterpillar

Children love to take a deep breath, unwind, and relax with this easy exercise known as progressive muscular relaxation. The technique focuses awareness on various muscle groups to create a complete resting of the mind and body.

A Boy and a Turtle
Children visualize filling their bodies with the colors of the rainbow. This gentle visualization technique relaxes the body and mind while boosting creativity. Kids love to play with colors.

A Boy and a Bear
Children follow the boy and bear as they learn to focus on their breathing to relax and self-regulate.

Affirmation Web
Children learn how to recite positive statements with the forest animals to improve confidence and self-esteem.

Many of our stories and *Sueños del océano indigo* CD are now available in Spanish.

ABOUT THE AUTHOR

Stress Free Kids® founder Lori Lite has created a line of books, CDs, and a curriculum designed to help children, teens, and adults decrease stress, anxiety, and anger. Her own experiences with stress sent her searching for techniques that people could utilize in their everyday lives. Her books, CDs, and lesson plans are considered a resource for parents, psychologists, therapists, child life specialists, teachers, yoga instructors, and doctors. Lori has been nationally recognized on programs such as *Shark Tank* and *CBS News*. Her sought-after practical tips and articles can be found in hundreds of publications such as *Family Circle*, *USA Today*, *Real Simple Magazine*, *Modern Mom*, the *New York Times*, and *Dr. Sears*. Her constant upbeat presence on Pinterest, Facebook, and Twitter @StressFreeKids make her tips real-time and accessible for today's parents. Her titles are available in Spanish and will also be released in Japan, Turkey, and South Korea.

INDEX